THE BATTLE FOR THE HEARTS AND MINDS OF MEN

SOVEREIGNTY

RYAN MICHLER

DEDICATION

To my wife, Tricia; my sons, Brecken, Eli, and Otto; and my daughter, Vivian. I may be my own man, but I wouldn't be the man I am without you. You are the reason this is my life's work.

ACKNOWLEDGEMENTS

I would be lying if I said I was able to accomplish the writing of this book on my own. The fact is, I could not have done without the support, guidance, and direction of countless men and women who have encouraged me to share the message within the pages of this book.

I want to thank Sandy Smith for cleaning up the words and thoughts I failed to adequately express. It's because of her, the message is clear, concise, and coherent.

I also want to express my gratitude to my designer, Juan Eddards, for making this work look so good. I fear the words I used to express my ideas won't live up to the quality of work he's done in making this a book you'll be proud to hold.

To my publisher, Jesse Krieger, and his team at Lifestyle Entrepreneurs Press, you've done an amazing job in keeping this project on track. I'm not sure there's another team out there that could have met the timetable and quality we worked so hard to create.

And, to my brothers inside the Iron Council, you will never fully know how much I appreciate you. This, quite literally, would have been impossible without you. You are among the few who have always believed in me and for that, I am eternally grateful.

Lastly, I want to thank the countless men who have gone before me and who are leading the charge in reclaiming what it means to be a man. You are leading from the front. You are forging new paths, and forgotten ones. You are exemplifying the Sovereign Man.

TABLE OF CONTENTS

INTRODUCTION

"The sovereignty of one's self over one's self is called liberty."
-Albert Pike

Sovereignty (noun): the quality or state of having supreme power or authority.

What is sovereignty? Perhaps it's better to start by illustrating what sovereignty is *not*. To do that, you don't have to look very far. Take a walk around your neighborhood. Take a stroll around your office. Have a conversation with your buddies. Everywhere you look, you'll find the signs of men who have neglected their responsibilities as men and, in turn, have given up their sovereignty or, in other words, the power they inherently have to control the outcome of their lives.

These men are no longer in control of their hearts and minds. They've traded their individual liberty and personal responsibility for a decent marriage, a steady paycheck, and a relatively painless life. In doing so, they have unknowingly enslaved themselves to their marriages, their jobs, and their governments.

The shackles they willingly submit themselves to are hard to quantify (if they were easily spotted, men wouldn't be so willing to give up their freedoms). These shackles come in the form of a marriage with "potential," a fancy 401(k) and retirement package, and the promise of safety and security in exchange for just a small percentage of their paycheck.

A man who has given up his sovereignty fabricates excuses. He tells himself stories. He feeds himself lies.

All of this to justify the reality that he has given away the one thing that has the potential to allow him to be the man he is meant to be: his sovereignty.

Unfortunately, it's easy to maintain the status quo. After all, the truth—that we are living in a cloud of delusion magnified by a silent attack on the very traits that make us men—is hard to bear.

This cloud of delusion makes everything *feel* real. We feel as if we command our minds, follow our heart, and take control of our bodies. We feel as if we're in charge, but ultimately we are being controlled and manipulated by some outside force we can't quite seem to see or understand.

But if we look deeper, beyond the thick cloud of delusion, we already know that, don't we? We can feel it lingering in the back of our consciousness. We can't yet wrap our heads around it, but we know it's there.

The first step toward sovereignty is to lift the cloud of delusion. It's not easy. It's not pleasant. But it's a necessity if you have any chance of overcoming the nagging thought that your life is not your own or that you know you're destined for more but don't know quite how to wrap heart, mind, and hands around it.

This is about control. This is about ownership. This is about facing the ugly reality that *you* aren't as good as you think you are and that the life you live today is not the one you're meant to live.

The answer to regaining control of yourself and lifting the cloud of delusion we all experience is the victory that lies only in becoming a Sovereign Man.

A SOVEREIGN MAN

A man who has battled for and reclaimed his sovereignty is a man who has decided to take ownership of his life and everything in it. This man recognizes that, although the world would have him believe otherwise, he has certain responsibilities. The only way to fully fulfill those responsibilities is to be the master of his life.

A Sovereign Man protects himself, his loved ones, and those who cannot protect themselves. He provides—not just financially, but emotionally, mentally, and spiritually as well. He presides in that he leads himself, his family, and his community.

It is painfully obvious that the Sovereign Man is becoming a rare breed. Take a look around society and you'll see the results of a lack of Sovereign Men.

The family unit is under attack. More and more young men and women are growing up without fathers. Crime is running rampant. Businesses are failing. Leadership at every level—from the home to the boardroom to the city, state, and national government—is all but nonexistent.

It seems the plague of men who are more interested in shirking their responsibilities for the path of least resistance is growing by the day, and Sovereign Men are becoming an increasing rarity.

Stepping through the cloud of delusion into the truth that you are called to be not just a man but a Sovereign Man is not an easy task. I know because I'm on the battlefield with you. I have two businesses to run. I have a wife to lead with. I have four kids who require me to be the type of man to which I'm referring. Add to that community service, spiritual obligations, and the endless requests for my time, and the task becomes nearly impossible.

It seems that making ends meet, keeping a roof over our heads and food on the table, coupled with the infinite number of obligations I have is never-ending. How is it possible for me to focus on myself and regain, at least to some degree, my own sovereignty?

In order to recapture your sovereignty, you're going to need to understand the first truth I want to share with you: as important as it is to fulfill your manly responsibility to others, it's imperative that you learn to take care of yourself. Because, at the end of the day, a man is responsible and accountable to himself first, *then* to the people he has an obligation to.

And that is the essence of what it means to be a Sovereign Man: maintaining accountability and responsibility to yourself.

Unfortunately, I didn't always live my life this way.

LIFTING THE CLOUD OF DELUSION

In October 2008, I had given away my sovereignty. The result was a broken man sobbing alone in a cold, dark room of the house my wife and I had built two years earlier.

In that room, I was hanging on to a memory of the family I had driven away. It was a picture of my six-month-old son. Through my tears I told the boy in that picture, "I will find a way to get you back."

Leading up to that event, I had spent two years giving away my sovereignty—and all the power that goes with it—to my wife, my employer, the economy, my father, the government, and anyone and anything else that placed itself between what I wanted and where I currently was. The demise of my sovereignty manifested itself in the lies and excuses I had fabricated to justify my lackluster business, my poor health, and my failing marriage.

I didn't believe it could possibly have anything to do with me. I'm a man. I'm *the* man. I'm supposed to have this all figured out. Yet, there I was with my business, my marriage, and my world crumbling around me. I was alone in a dark room, broken by the world I had created for myself (or, more accurately, what I had given away to others).

Just a few days earlier my wife and I had gotten into an argument. I can't tell you what it was about. I'm sure it wasn't anything worth fighting over, but the months and years of disagreements and discontent had come to a boiling point that evening when the words "I don't even want to be married to you anymore" slipped out of my mouth.

She agreed. And the next day she was gone.

"How could she do this to me?" I thought.

"How could she be so disloyal?"

"How could she take my son away from me?"

"Why didn't she appreciate what I did for the family?"

"Why wasn't she doing the things a good wife should do?"

I asked myself those questions. I said those things to myself, and worse.

And for a long time, I blamed her. It had to be her fault. It couldn't *possibly* be mine. I was the man, after all. I was bringing home an income. I was growing a business. I had bought her a home. I had served my country as a soldier in Iraq.

From the outside, I was doing it all right. I had this all figured out. But it become apparent that I did not. I don't remember why or how, but as I was on a drive one day, I came to a conclusion and a revelation that would alter the course of my marriage, my business, and my life.

For the first time during my separation with my wife, I told myself the truth that our marriage might be over. And, if that was the case, as much as I hated to admit it, I resolved to be the greatest catch for the next woman to come into my life.

That's when it all clicked for me. I had been blaming *her*. But what I failed to realize is that as I was blaming her, I was simultaneously giving her all the power I had once possessed to make something of myself. You see, if it was her fault, then all I could do was *wait* for her to do something about it. And that is why I felt so powerless. I was.

The moment I began to accept responsibility for my part in the demise of our relationship, the more I began to wrestle control back in my life. The more I faced the reality that I was inadequate in our marriage, my business, and my life, the more I gave myself the power to do something about it.

When I stopped focusing on her and, instead, decided to focus on myself, she responded to *me*. I still remember the day she called me and told me she wanted to come back home.

That was nine years ago. This year marks our thirteenth anniversary. We have four incredible children and two thriving businesses. We make more money than we ever have. I'm stronger and healthier than I've ever been. And we literally have the white-picket fence (I put it up myself a couple of months ago).

Things aren't easy. We don't live the perfect life. She and I still disagree from time to time. My businesses have their ups and downs. But I have created a roadmap for taking ownership, power, and control of my own life—for wrestling back my heart and mind.

I took the concepts I learned when working through my failing marriage and applied them to my health, relationships, finances, and every other facet of my life. Whether you're trying to save your marriage (as I was), grow a business, lose thirty extra pounds, secure a job promotion, or build your bank account, what follows in these pages is the roadmap for making that a reality—for becoming a Sovereign Man.

It's not an easy path. It's not the fast track. It's a painstaking process that will take you years—and a lot of blood, sweat, and tears—to implement. If that's something you're not willing to accept, I'd encourage you to put this book down and keep making excuses and giving away all your power.

If, on the other hand, you're ready for a change and ready to do the work required to see it through, the information contained in this book will show you how. It all starts with you, the Sovereign Man. The good news is you already have everything you need. We just need to uncover it.

PART I

THE BATTLE

"Every normal man must be tempted, at times, to spit on his hands, hoist the black flag, and begin slitting throats."
-H.L Mencken

Make no mistake, we are at war. Every time we get out of bed. Every time we go in to work. Every time we engage with those we care about. Every time we're called to complete a task. It is a battle.

But it's a battle worth fighting. It's a noble cause. If won, the battle will lead to tremendous success on every front for yourself and those you care about. If lost, it will lead to a life of complacency, mediocrity, dissatisfaction, and discontent.

Some may argue that using the word "battle" is sensational. I agree. But I use the word intentionally. Too many men have taken a passive approach to their lives and, in turn, have created a life they're not at all proud of living. If framing every waking hour of your day as a battle gives you the power to wrestle back control of your life, that's the word I'm going to use, sensational or not.

That aside, taking control of your life will have its fair share of challenges. It wouldn't be worth it if it didn't. The difference between all the experiences I remember and the ones I don't are those memories of hardship, struggle, trial, and adversity.

Sure, it would be nice to live in a world where we never had to test ourselves—but only for a while. Truth be told, we, as men, are built to fight. Physically, mentally, and emotionally. When we remove the need for battle in our lives, we strip away all the qualities that make us men in the first place: anger, aggression, rage, violence, dominance, and strength.

Unfortunately, we've been told those qualities are to be shunned and that we should be embarrassed of the desire to be this kind of man. So, in a misguided attempt to keep society safe and free from conflict, the warrior within us has been silenced. Silenced by our school systems, the government, the media, our friends and family, and, unfortunately, ourselves.

You can feel it, right? I know I can. For too long I sat silently by as I was conditioned to believe that men should "sit down, shut up, and do what we're told." Only when society is in trouble (conflict, natural disaster, etc.) are we given "permission" to be the kind of men we know we are meant to be. It's as if we have been caged and leashed and only called upon when needed.

But what if there was a better way? What if there was a way to take all that we already are and harness that power to become all we are meant to be?

There is. This is the battle I'm talking about. It's a battle for your Sovereignty. It's real. It's brutal. And it's exciting. John Eldredge, author of *Wild at Heart*, says, "Deep in his heart, every man longs for a battle to fight, an adventure to live, and a beauty to rescue." There is something calling to you. It calls to every man. It's the sound of battle. Although we may define our battles differently, *every* man hears the battle drums.

If you have any hope of winning this battle, you must be equipped with the tools required to thrive. You must recognize the situation in which you find yourself. You must recognize the enemy. You must make a choice to either enter the fray or continue to watch life pass you by.

CHAPTER 1

THE SITUATION

"The mass of men lead lives of quiet desperation."
-Henry David Thoreau

There was a time in my life when I was the very man Henry David Thoreau was talking about when he said, "The mass of men lead lives of quiet desperation." I was fifty pounds overweight, my marriage was in shambles, my finances were a wreck, and my mind was lost in a sea of negativity and overwhelmed at the position I found myself in. As I began to share my story of personal failure and setback with the men closest to me, I began to see a disturbing trend: most men, although they were good at masking it, were *also* leading lives of desperation.

Take one metric, the alarming rate of suicide in men today (one study suggested that suicide rates among men are up to three times higher than that of women), and you'll understand how bad it really is. Odds are that you or someone you know is experiencing anxiety, depression, and suicidal thoughts. What makes matters worse is that there is an unwritten rule that says you and I, as men, are not supposed to talk about our weaknesses, struggles, and shortcomings.

For as long as history can remember, it has been the man's responsibility to have everything figured out. When things go wrong, everyone looks to the man. When there's no money coming into the household, people look to the man. When there's an emergency or disaster, people look to the man.

Makes sense, right? We are supposed to have it all figured out. We're men, after all. And if we don't have things under control, we'll be led to believe we're not as manly as we're supposed to be.

So, we walk around with a happy face. We puff out our chests. We put up a wall. And we pretend. We pretend we don't have emotions. We pretend nothing gets to us. We pretend we have it all figured out. The reality, however, is an entirely different story.

ISOLATION

That reality is that we're lonely. What's interesting is, that last sentence was hard for me to write. Why? Because men aren't supposed to be lonely. We're supposed to be the lone wolf, the sole leader, the "alpha."

But deep down we want to be able to talk about our struggles. We want other men to bounce ideas off. We want someone to help us be accountable. We want to join the battle for our lives with our brothers in arms.

Unfortunately, we bought into the idea that reaching out for guidance, direction, and brotherhood isn't manly at all. We started to believe the notion of the "self-made man" was the highest achievement any man could obtain.

Consider James Bond and Jason Bourne. These men are the epitome of perceived masculinity: strong, knowledgeable, charismatic, and *alone*.

What looks good on the silver screen, however, doesn't really play out. When we attempt to isolate ourselves and shield our experiences, thoughts, and emotions from others, we limit our growth and expansion.

Our ancestors knew this. For as long as men have been on this planet, we've been forming packs and tribes. They knew that if they had any hope of survival, they would need to come together as an opportunity to accommodate each other's strengths and weaknesses, learn new ways of growing food and making war, and solidify their communities.

In his poem "The Law of the Jungle," Rudyard Kipling writes:

Now this is the Law of the Jungle—as old and as true as the sky;
And the Wolf that shall keep it may prosper, but the Wolf that shall break it must die.
As the creeper that girdles the tree-trunk the Law runneth forward and back—
For the strength of the Pack is the Wolf, and the strength of the Wolf is the Pack.

What Kipling means is that the pack (our friends, families, neighborhoods, and communities) is only as strong as the individual members of that pack (us), and the individual members of that pack are only as strong as the pack they live in.

Thousands of years ago, this was common knowledge, but today we are more disconnected than we have ever been, in spite of being closer in physical proximity than ever before.

I realize that as the risk of dying from a natural disaster, a medical emergency, or the hands of another man has declined, our need to congregate to stay safe and secure and to expand has declined. For the most part, gone are the days when we had to guard against attack by a neighboring tribe. Gone are the days when we ate only what we killed. Gone are the days when provisions were in short supply.

So, we disbanded. The result is millions of men who are left to walk alone, wallowing in their own self-pity, with no guidance, direction, or purpose, and, though surrounded by people every day, completely isolated from the world.

As Rudyard Kipling predicted, "the Wolf that shall break it must die." Although our isolation may not result in literal death, it's death all the same—the death of the hearts and minds of men.

UNDEFINED EXPECTATIONS

Thousands of years ago, there wasn't a whole lot of guesswork with regard to what our role was as men. We were expected to hunt. We were expected to defend our tribes. We were expected to lead our people. Of course, times have changed and become significantly more complex. With the added level of complexity in our lives, we've been left wondering how and where we fit into society.

As I was running an errand the other day, I looked over to another car while I was stopped at a stoplight. I saw a man driving a mini-van with his wife in the passenger seat. His wife was turned around to face the three children in the back. She was yelling at them, and I could see that the children were a bit excited, to say the least. I looked back at the man and couldn't help but wonder what was going through his mind as I watched his expressionless face staring through the windshield. It was as if this man had been somehow replaced with a lifeless robot or the shell of the man who once sat in his place. Maybe he was just tired.

Either way, what I recognized that day was a man who had lost who he was and why he was here. In the work I do, I hear from men every day who are confused about what exactly they should be doing.

In my experience, when a man becomes so confused about what his purpose on this planet is, he stops. He disengages. This is what I recognized in the man driving next to me.

It's easy to understand why this happens. Look around for just a minute and you'll see that more and more, the role of men is being undermined and undervalued. Men are mocked by the media in movies and television. We're portrayed as a threat to the overall existence of humanity. Our school systems are stacked against young men. Increasingly so, our boys are being raised by women. Even the Boy Scouts have begun to deteriorate as they move away from the mission of serving boys to making their programs more inclusive to young ladies.

But heaven forbid you bring that up. You'll get slaughtered. Every time I make mention of the fight for our young men, I'm met with resistance and insults that range from cries of sexism to misogyny.

It seems the only time men are valued is when there is some sort of emergency we are uniquely qualified to handle. No one complained about masculinity when Houston was in disarray from Hurricane Harvey. Story after story began to unfold as thousands of men poured into the city with the boats, tools, and skills required to relieve the people of Texas.

I could share countless stories of men who step up to the plate when needed where no one bats an eye. But in times of relative peace and security, masculinity is once again under attack from the misinformed and misguided. Like the axe that sits in the case on the wall under a label that says IN CASE OF EMERGENCY, BREAK GLASS, men are sidelined until society deems them useful.

We ask women to raise our young men (and bless their hearts, they do the best they can), but there are certain things a woman can never teach a young man, just as there are things a man could never teach a young woman. We condition boys to be quiet, ask why they aren't performing as well as girls, and strip away all the qualities that make them male—then have the audacity to ask where all the real men have gone.

We're still here. But we've hardened our hearts, we've put away the things that make us men, and, in a way, we've given the proverbial middle finger to a society that doesn't appreciate what we bring to the table.

And the cycle perpetuates.

OUR OWN WORST ENEMY

I could sit here and continue to write about the assault on masculinity. I could write a book that blames everything and everyone for our misfortunes as men. But that isn't the kind of book I'm interested in writing, and it isn't reality.

Sure, there are some things stacked against us, but that's never deterred us from taking on a challenge anyway. In fact, men thrive when faced with a challenge. We're built to step up when the odds are against us.

This isn't a book designed to make you feel like a victim of society's agenda. This is a book about taking control of your life. In order to do that, you've got to recognize that you have control in the first place. You've got to recognize that as many challenges as we face, we tend to be our own worst enemy.

That's right, we get in our own way. We shoot ourselves in the foot. For all of society's problems, could it be that we have perpetuated some of them?

When I first started sharing my story, specifically the separation with my wife, I made a video that explained what had happened to us and how I came to the conclusion that much of what we went through was my fault. That video has been viewed hundreds of thousands of times, and I've received thousands of messages about it—some positive, some negative. The negative comments I've received bring to light something very interesting: it's hard for a lot of us to accept Sovereignty of our lives.

I've been called a cuck. I've been called a beta. I've been called a pussy. I've been called pathetic. I've been called every name under the sun following the release of that video. Why these names and comments?

Simply because I admitted that much of the demise of my relationship with my wife was my fault.

"Well, Ryan, it takes two to tango."

"She had something to do with it as well."

And, my personal favorite, "You're the problem with society because you take on too much responsibility and make yourself subservient to women."

It's an interesting perspective but wrong nonetheless. It's *because* I'm willing to accept my share of the fault that I make myself subservient to nothing and no one. It's *because* I recognize that I am weak that I become the master of my soul. It's *because* I see that I am my own worst enemy that I gain my Sovereignty.

There is nothing so damaging to the hearts and minds of men as ourselves. There is a far greater enemy that lies within us than lies outside of us. He's called the Natural Man.

The Natural Man is weak. The Natural Man is a coward. The Natural Man is lazy. The Natural Man is a liar, a cheat, and a thief. The Natural Man wants something for nothing. The Natural Man is pathetic.

Unfortunately, the Natural Man is within us all, and in order to become a Sovereign Man, you're going to have to battle yourself, your greatest enemy.

It's easy to see yourself as a victim. It's infinitely harder to see that, in many cases, we've made ourselves the victim. Why do we do this? Why do we cling so hard to the role of victim? Again, it's easy.

If you acknowledge that you are not a victim and that many of the negative circumstances you find yourself in are your fault, the result means effort. After all, if it's someone else's fault, there's nothing you can do. If it's your fault, there is.

The Natural Man doesn't like to exert effort. He wants things to be easy. He wants things to be safe. He wants things to be comfortable. And as good as that may sound, ease, safety, and comfort are directly at odds with your Sovereignty.

You've created many of your own problems. Your marriage isn't perfect, not because society is attacking the family, but because you've refused to do the work required to build a thriving marriage. You didn't get the promotion, not because your boss is out to get you, but because you refused to exert the effort required to secure the promotion. You gained an extra fifty pounds, not because there wasn't a gym near you, but because you actually believed that's what was keeping you back.

You've shot yourself in the foot and now you're blaming other people. You should be blaming the man in the mirror: the Natural Man.

Sovereignty requires you to take off the blindfold. Regardless of what your mommy and daddy have been telling you, you aren't perfect. Regardless of the lies you've told yourself, you aren't as good as you think you are. Regardless of the battle that society has waged on men, *you* are your greatest enemy.

This truth will threaten some men. They'll go on the defensive. They'll continue to post negative comments about my shortcomings while refusing to look at their own. They'll say I've made myself a beta or slave to others while they've become slaves themselves.

For the rest of you, the thought that you are your own worst enemy will be empowering. You recognize there isn't much you can do about outside factors, but you're ready to take on the battle with yourself.

CHAPTER 2

THE CHOICE

"Neither a wise man nor a brave man lies down on the tracks of history to wait for the train of the future to run over him."
-Dwight D. Eisenhower

You have a choice to make. Do you stick your head in the sand and pretend everything is normal, or do you step into the unknown, face the reality of your own inadequecies, and give yourself the chance to become something more?

I think we already know the answer to that question or you wouldn't be here. You wouldn't have purchased this book. You wouldn't be listening to our podcast. You wouldn't belong to the Order of Man or the Iron Council.

But let's be honest, those things are easy, right? It's easy to listen to a podcast on the way to a job you don't enjoy. It's easy to read a few pages of a book and get hyped up, then do nothing. It's easy to join one of our Facebook groups, make a few posts, and pretend you've got this whole "being a better man" thing figured out. It's easy to put on the dog-and-pony show your wife, kids, and friends expect you to put on. It's easy to go to a few conferences, make a few changes for a few days, then revert back to the status quo.

The choice I'm asking you to make is not, however, an easy one. I'm asking you to make real and lasting changes in your life. I'm asking you to commit not for the next ninety days, but for a lifetime of wrestling control of your own sovereignty.

Along this journey, you're going to have to face some hard truths you may have been hiding for years. There may be some serious conversations you'll need to have. There will be some challenges and activities you're going to want to resist.

We've got to be realistic about what it will take or you'll quit before you give yourself a chance to succeed. One of my friends and mentors, Sean Whalen, says, "Radical change requires radical change."

Are you willing to radically change your life, or are you just paying it lip service? If it's lip service, put this book down, send me a message, and lie about all the wonderful things you're now going to do with your life since reading the book, then go on doing the same thing in your life—lying to others and lying to yourself.

I understand your hesitancy. Some of you might be saying, "Let me just see what Ryan has to say, then I'll decide." Look, change is not an easy thing. You may be completely unhappy with your life. Your marriage might be in shambles. Your career may be nonexistent. Your health may be deteriorating. And still you refuse to change.

I get it. Change is scary. And it's risky.

RISK

As a financial advisor, it's my job to understand risk. Market risk, political risk, legislative risk, credit risk, liquidity risk, on and on and on.

Most of us spend our entire lives trying to avoid risk. What a shame, since, with as much uncertainty as there is, there is no way to remove risk fully from our lives.

Why should we attempt to remove it anyway? Some of the most amazing events in the history of the world have involved risk. Discovery of new lands, America's independence from Great Britain, putting a man on the moon, and so many more all involved significant levels of risk.

Since risk cannot be eliminated altogether, the notion that we should avoid it at all costs is absurd. No, the goal should not be to *remove* risk but rather to take *calculated* risk.

When I talk with my financial advisory clients, we don't talk about removing risk first; we talk about what risk they're willing to take relative to the return they hope to receive. The same idea holds true as you are considering embarking on a journey that has the potential to change your life for the better.

See, right now, with your current beliefs, thoughts, and actions, you might be living with the false idea that somehow you're safe. You may not put it that way, but if you believed you were in danger, you would do something different. It's part of the human condition—to look for risk and to remove it from your life.

But what if I were to tell you that the greater risk lies not in doing something new but in maintaining the status quo? If you continue to bury your head in the sand and refuse to do the work necessary to recapture and maintain your Sovereignty, you're opening yourself up to all sorts of blind spots that could potentially derail you.

You think you're safe now because the reality of doing nothing hasn't caught up with you yet. But when it does, it will come with a vengeance. On that day, ignorance is not a successful defense strategy.

With my investment clients, the most successful investors are those who make the decision to be proactive in their approach to the markets. You too must be proactive in your approach to your life. And make no mistake, being proactive does not mean being active; it simply means you're willing to take an objective look at the data and information with an open heart and an open mind and act accordingly.

I think you probably already know if you're willing to do that or not. But before I ask you to choose, let me share one more thing with you.

COMPLACENCY KILLS

In 2005–2006, I spent a year of my life in Ramadi, Iraq, which was, at the time, the hotbed for the remaining insurgency during Operation Iraqi Freedom.

The first time I walked into the adobe building that would become my office, I noticed fourteen pictures of soldiers hanging on the wall. I asked one of the officers, "What are these pictures on the wall?"

As it turned out, those were pictures of the fourteen soldiers that unit had lost while they were serving their deployment. Obviously, this was a very sobering experience, considering we were going in to replace them.

As we served our time in Iraq, we adopted many mantras, one of which was "complacency kills." As in, literal death. If you didn't show up on time to your post or didn't give all of your energy and attention or got a little careless or slacked off in any number of situations that could happen, you or a brother or sister in arms ran the very real risk of dying on the battlefield.

If that was the case, one father was not going home to see his son play baseball. One husband was not going home to be with his wife. One man was not going home to lead in his community.

I know what it's like to play for keeps. And, in the context of war, it's easy to say that you would always be on your game, that you'd always show up focused, and that you would always do your job at a hundred percent.

We didn't lose a single soldier from our unit while we were deployed to Iraq. There were some close calls and there were men and women stationed on our base who died, but not one from our unit. We were fortunate. We were anything but complacent.

That said, most of us haven't played a game of life and death. Most of us, if we become complacent, we lose our jobs or get sued or separate from our wife. We don't die. Perhaps if the stakes were higher, we'd recognize that the complacency with which we've been living is not an adequate way to live at all.

In 2008, I hit rock bottom. As I mentioned previously, my wife had left with my six-month-old son, I was in horrible physical shape, my business was atrophying, and I was miserable. It took a serious jolt to wake me from the slumber I had found myself in. I can't help but wonder if I would have needed to hit rock bottom at all if I'd have adopted our military mantra—"complacency kills"— in my civilian life.

Do any of us need to hit rock bottom before we wake up? You may have already hit the bottom. You may not have yet. Either way, what you do now is up to you.

WHAT WILL YOU DO?

Newton's First Law of Motion states, "An object at rest stays at rest and an object in motion stays in motion with the same speed and in the same direction unless acted upon by an unbalanced force."

What is the unbalanced force that will get you moving? A divorce, a separation, a layoff, a bankruptcy, a heart attack? Or can it be something significantly less drastic, like this book for example?

The difference between you and an inanimate object is that you don't need to be "acted upon" in order to change course. You can simply decide to change. Most men won't. It requires time. It requires energy. It requires resources. And it requires effort.

But you're different. That's why you're reading this book. You know there's something more out there. You know that you are meant to make more of your life. You're not comfortable with maintaining the status quo.

Although you know there's more out there, you just can't quite put your finger on it. We're going to help you with that, but in order for you to do it, you have to make a decision. Most people want the results without the effort. In a way, by asking for the answer before they've earned it, they're attempting to remove the risk of uncertainty from their lives. This is not like that, and this will not be like most journeys.

You have to commit first. Then, and only then, will you experience the results. If you can't commit, put on the blindfold you took off long enough to read up to this point and do what you've always done.

Sure, you'll continue to experience the same results and the sense of frustration that comes with stagnation, but on the bright side, you'll get to stay in your bubble. You'll get to stay comfortable. You won't have to do hard things. You won't have to push yourself. You won't subject yourself to ridicule, judgment, and the loss of friends and family who aren't interested in seeing you change.

On the other hand, you could decide that you're no longer going to live what Teddy Roosevelt refers to as "a life of ease and comfort." You're not going to live in complacency. You're going to decide that the blindfold you've been wearing has been taken off for good.

If this is the case, you're ready for more. You're willing to do the work required to have more in your life. You understand that it's not going to be easy. It's not going to be comfortable. At times you're going to be scared, confused, and about ready to throw in the towel. But you won't, because you are ready to play for keeps—ready to take charge of your business and employment, ready to take charge of and responsibility for the relationships you're working to build, ready to take care of your body the way it's meant to be taken care of, and ready to take care of every facet of your life.

First, let's talk about what this path looks like, then we'll begin.

CHAPTER 3

THE PATH

"Sad will be the day for any man when he becomes contented with the thoughts he is thinking and the deeds he is doing - where there is not forever beating at the doors of his soul some great desire to do something larger; which he knows he was meant and made to do."
-Phillips Brooks

Congratulate yourself for making a wise choice that will positively impact you, your family, your friends, your neighborhood, your community, and your posterity.

Get ready to open your eyes to some information you may never have heard before—or never heard in this way— and free yourself from the delusion that you've been living in. Most men never come to the conclusion that you have. They're afraid. So afraid that it causes them to shrink in fear of what has the power to change their lives. You might be experiencing that fear now. You might be asking yourself some questions.

"What if I have to do something different?" You will.

"What if some people don't like who I will have to become?" They won't.

"What if I lose some friendships along the way?" It's going to happen.

You have to come to terms with that in order to implement the changes I'm going to ask you to make. It's not easy, but neither is living as a slave to the circumstances you've created for yourself up to this point. Coming to terms with the fact that you are going to push yourself outside of your current comfort zone, answer some tough questions from family and friends, and potentially alienate those closest to you does nothing to eliminate the fear.

You're probably still afraid (maybe more so), but the pain of staying where you currently are has become greater than the fear that remains. That's why you're still with me.

So potentially, for the first time in your life, you've decided to take a stand. For the first time in your life, you might be saying to yourself, "enough is enough."

For the first time in your life, you are no longer interested in living beholden to your boss, your wife, your family, your body, or anyone or anything else that has been keeping you back from the life you, as a man, are meant to live.

So, where do we go from here?

THE MISSION

Before you understand *how* to regain your sovereignty, you need to understand *why* it's important you do it in the first place. Up to this point we've talked about the delusion you've been living in. We've talked about the nagging feeling of uncertainty you may be experiencing. We've talked about the power and feeling that come with the liberation of your heart and mind.

At the end of the day, it really isn't worth it (or even necessary) to regain your Sovereignty if there isn't some purpose you have for being alive in the first place. And it's my belief that all men have a mission on this planet. Without a mission, men wander around aimlessly, wondering when they're going to catch their break. They may look around and see other men operating with focus and clarity and wonder why they seem to lack that in their life. In many cases, the missing piece is an understanding of why we're here and what we're here to do. Only then, when we have the mission, can we truly begin the journey.

Men have a responsibility on this planet, just as women have a responsibility. In many cases, these responsibilities overlap, and how men fulfill their calling may differ, but every man's mission is to protect, provide, and preside. This basic understanding provides the foundation and framework for the Sovereignty we're working to capture.

Many people have tried to make me believe differently about why I'm here, but the more I bring my beliefs and action in line with the noble calling of protector, provider, and presider, the more content, confident, and satisfied I am. No man can fully be Sovereign who does not have goals, ambitions, and a desire to fulfill the mission of stepping into the noble calling that defines a man.

In Part II, we'll break down the three-point mission Sovereign Men engage in and teach you how you can be fully the protector, provider, and presider others rely on you to be, and, more importantly, a man who operates with clarity, purpose, and direction.

THE CODE OF CONDUCT

In Part III, we'll break down the Code of Conduct every Sovereign Man lives by. Consider this code as an operating system by which you can judge your thoughts, ideas, actions, and interactions on a daily basis. Every great society and every great man has a set of rules or guidelines by which he lives his life.

Consider this excerpt from the U.S. Army Soldier's Creed:

> I am disciplined, physically and mentally tough, trained and proficient in my warrior tasks and drills.
> I always maintain my arms, my equipment and myself.

I am an expert and I am a professional.

I stand ready to deploy, engage, and destroy, the enemies of the United States of America in close combat.

Or the Navy SEAL Code:

- Loyalty to Country, Team and Teammate
- Serve with Honor and Integrity On and Off the Battlefield
- Ready to Lead, Ready to Follow, Never Quit
- Take responsibility for your actions and the actions of your teammates
- Excel as Warriors through Discipline and Innovation
- Train for War, Fight to Win, Defeat our Nation's Enemies
- Earn your Trident everyday

The code we discuss in Part III comprises the components of the Sovereign Man's Creed: Self-Reliance, Intentionality, Discernment, Wisdom, Ownership, Strength, Humility, Integrity, Conviction, Self-Awareness, Discipline, Mastery, and Courage.

It is critical that you internalize this code. As you are faced with the challenges that will inevitably arise as you wrestle for control of your life, you need an operating system by which to measure your decisions.

In his book *On Killing*, Colonel Grossman discusses the idea that we must come up with a set of predetermined responses so when we're faced with difficult decisions, we don't allow the filter of emotions we're looking through to taint our ability and desire to make the right choice.

Knowing, understanding, and internalizing the Code of Conduct will help you make definitive decisions in the midst of difficult circumstances.

THE BATTLE PLAN

What good is all this information if you don't know how to use it effectively in your life?

In Part IV, we begin to bridge the gap between what you know you should be doing and what you're *actually* doing.

Frankly speaking, we are not at a loss for information. We have access to information on a scale the world has never seen. Yet we, as men, continue to make the same decisions that have produced results less than we're capable of. Why the disparity? Why do we continue to do the exact opposite of what we know we should be doing? The answer: we have no plan for incorporating all that we learn.

Information is the simple part, and up until now, you may be thinking, "This doesn't sound too bad. I can recapture my sovereignty quickly and painlessly." If information was all you needed, though, we'd all be millionaires with chiseled six-pack abs. Everyone knows how to get wealthy: add more value to the marketplace, spend less money. Everyone knows how to get healthier: eat less, move more.

Even with access to all the knowledge in the world, we may *still* find ourselves with too much month at the end of the money and a few extra pounds around the midsection.

With that in mind, Part IV is designed to walk you through an effective Battle Plan and arm you with the tools, the resources, and the information to actually make the information and application of it stick. Not only are we going to walk you through the process of building a Battle Plan, we're going to help you build your own. By the time you're done with this book, you'll have a crystal-clear course of action moving forward.

ENGAGE

Everything you will have read up to this point will be absolutely useless unless you engage—unless you implement what you have learned.

Most people fail in execution, not understanding. When I started the Order of Man in 2015, I did not intend to start a movement of information no one had ever heard of before.

In fact, everything I have ever said and ever shared has already been said and shared before. Sure, I may have put a new spin on it, but the fact remains, none of this is new information.

You, the reader of this book, already know what to do. But for some reason, there is a disconnect between what you know you should be doing and what you *actually* do. For example, if I told you to give me the basic principles of weight loss, what would you say? Eat less, move more. How about the principles of building wealth? Buy low, sell high. How about the principles of building a successful relationship? Give more than you take.

Pretty simple, right? But not so simple in application. The last thing I want is to create a good-looking book with some temporarily motivating rhetoric. I want to create something that will be the genesis of a new direction in your life—a lifelong commitment to the application of Sovereignty.

So, I'm going to issue you some challenges. I'm going to ask you to put into practice all that I have shared and all that you have been doing up to this point. I'm going to ask you to identify some of the challenges that will inevitably rear their ugly heads. And face it all on your feet and drive on. With the information that follows in these pages, you will have the knowledge, tools, and skills to do just that.

Let's get started.

PART II

THE MISSION

"I submit to you that if a man hasn't discovered something he will die for, he isn't fit to live."
-Martin Luther King Jr.

Before we move any further, it's critical we understand that a Sovereign Man does not operate at a disregard for others. If anything, a Sovereign Man battles for his sovereignty so that he may *serve* others more effectively.

There seems to be a growing trend in society that men operate independently of and without care for others. A relatively new movement called Men Going Their Own Way (MGTOW) has sprung up as an unhealthy and unnatural response by men who have become too dependent on or hurt by women.

Where Sovereignty is reserved for men who take control of their lives in order to more fully fulfill their responsibilities, commitments, and obligations to themselves and others, MGTOW and similar movements are more concerned with alienating themselves from women and potentially society altogether.

That's not at all what this is about. Sovereignty is about positioning yourself in a way that equips you with the mindset and skill set required to protect, provide, and preside—your true calling as a man. And, interestingly enough, it's in the service of others that we come alive as men as we have been biologically programmed to carry out this mission.

In order to take off the blindfold you've been wearing and regain control of your heart and mind, you need to understand *why* you're doing it in the first place. If you don't, this difficult journey won't stick, and you'll revert to the path you've always traveled.

After all is said and done, it is my hope you will see that this is your job and that others are relying upon you to step into this calling. But equally important is the sense of pride, power, and satisfaction a man feels when he is doing what he was born to do. This is the missing link between men who feel lost and confused about who they are and why they're here and those with a clear understanding of their role as men.

I haven't always lived by this mission. For a long time I floundered when it came to my role and responsibility as a man. The confusion in my life stemmed from spending most of my childhood without a father figure. (I don't, however, use this as an excuse. More on that later.)

When I was three years old, my father and mother split. When I was nine, a new man came into my life as my stepfather. Unfortunately, he was an alcoholic. He was never abusive, but he wasn't present the way a father should be. I remember glimpses of a healthy relationship with him. He would take us to the sprint car races, and we'd laugh and yell together as we watched the cars race around the dirt track. I also remember building Pinewood Derby cars together. In fact, I still have the two cars we built—one, deep maroon and the other, bright orange.

Before long, that marriage ended and, when I was thirteen years old, a new stepfather came into my life. This man, however, was verbally and emotionally abusive. He was very successful, very charismatic, and very confident, but he used those gifts and abilities to push people down rather than lift them up. He never treated me poorly; in fact, he treated me great. His anger and bitterness were directed at my mother and my sister.

I remember the day we left. My mom and stepfather argued; I'm not sure what their argument was about, but my mom grabbed my sister and me and we all ran out the door. The three of us ran into the garage, where he had disabled the car we were about to leave in. Apparently this had happened before, because my mom knew exactly what to do to get the car started again. As she fired up the car, he came running out of the house. She was so scared for her safety, as well as ours, that she drove through the garage door as he tried to shut it in order to keep us from leaving.

As we sped off, he chased us down the street and slammed on the passenger-side window—the side I was on. I did the only thing I could do at that point I tried to punch him through the window. I hit the window twice before it shattered onto the road and left my hand sliced and bloodied. I still have the scars to prove it.

Needless to say, I didn't have a great role model growing up. I didn't know how a man treated his wife and children. I didn't know how a man showed up in his career. I didn't know how a man showed up in his community.

Fortunately, my mother knew I would need the influence of good, strong men in my life. She got me involved in sports—specifically, baseball, football, and wrestling. It was there on the field where I learned what it meant to be a man. I learned from my coaches, who were disciplined, tough, and committed. They never took it easy on me or any of the other boys, but I never doubted that they cared for us and were equipping us with the tools and skills and code to succeed on the field and off.

The foundational element of the Sovereign experience is the understanding that you have a calling, an obligation, and a responsibility to fulfill: a mission. You are on this planet for a reason. I don't know what it is. You might not know what it is yet either. It's my goal to get you closer to discovering it.

Although there are many paths that lead to your calling as a man, you're here to protect, provide, and preside. Let me show you what that means.

CHAPTER 4

PROTECT

"The art of war teaches us to rely not on the likelihood of the enemy's not coming, but on our own readiness to receive him; not on the chance of his not attacking, but rather on the fact that we have made our position unassailable."
-Sun Tzu

Since the dawn of man we, as men, have answered the calling of protector. I don't take the word "calling" lightly. Whether you're a creationist or an evolutionist, it is very clear that biologically, we were meant to be protectors.

Generally speaking, men are bigger, faster, and stronger than women. That alone should be proof enough.

For thousands of years, we've been tapped to protect our tribes and watch over our people.

Some people seem to think that's no longer important or relevant. And, while the luxuries of modernity have drastically reduced the likelihood that we'll need to defend ourselves or our loved ones, it has become painfully obvious that the wicked of the world have preyed upon our weaknesses for too long.

Take the schoolyard bully who runs rampant because the school and legal system have made it all but impossible for one assertive child to punch him in his teeth. Rather than allow a young boy to handle the situation himself, the so-called solution is nothing more than a weak attempt to address the actual problem. We see ad campaigns designed to stop bullying "in the hopes," as one campaign ad says, "of preventing attacks on students." These cute little campaigns (one campaign I saw is called "Mean Stinks") would be great if little Johnny wasn't a punk who deserved to get knocked out.

Just the other day, my son told me he pushed a kid down at school. He did it in defense of his friend who was being picked on. I told him I was proud of him and congratulated him for doing the right thing. Two years ago he was being picked on in school. This year, he stands up for himself and others. Guess what? Nobody picks on him anymore.

Want to stop bullying for good? Teach your children not to be victims and step up as a protector to themselves and others.

On a more horrific note, take, for example, the self-righteous murderer who walks into a school, office building, or public space and shoots anything and anyone unfortunate enough to get in his path. Society's response? "It's not his fault. He had (insert excuse here)," or even more misguided, "Let's shower him with love."

Nice. What if the psychopath/mass murderer isn't interested in hugs, rainbows, and fairy tales? No, what we need are men who are adequately prepared, trained, and equipped to distribute consequences to the enemy of public and individual safety. That would be your job.

Before we go any further, let me be clear that I don't believe violence is always or even the *first* answer. Sometimes? Yes. Always? No. That said, and in the words of the well-known Chinese proverb, "It is better to be a warrior in the garden than a gardener in a war."

This book is by no means designed to teach you all you need to do to become the protector you're meant to be. There have been plenty of books written on the subjects I will briefly discuss. I do believe we should, at a minimum, discuss the elements every man should be aware of that, when *not* addressed, have the potential to limit your sovereignty and the sovereignty of those in your care.

This knowledge and understanding represents the first point of a man's mission: protect.

SITUATIONAL AWARENESS

Let's do an exercise. Go to a public space (restaurant, airport, park, etc.) and take a seat. Are you comfortable? Good. Now take a look around and start counting how many people have absolutely no clue what is going on around them and are completely oblivious to their surroundings. You'll find the vast majority of the people you observe have their noses stuck in their phones or are so entrenched in their activities that they wouldn't have any clue how many people are around them; who looks suspicious; what potential threats exist; where to find the nearest exit and/or escape route, cover, and concealment; or how to handle any other factor that could potentially keep them out of harm's way.

In his book *Left of Bang*, Patrick Van Horne illustrates Cooper's Color Code as a system for understanding and identifying patterns and the differing levels of awareness you should understand.

Condition White is described as unaware and unprepared. Condition Yellow is described as relaxed alert, with no specific threat situation. Condition Orange is described as specific alert—as something is not quite right and has your attention. Condition Red is described as response mode and on the offense/defense.

The goal of Cooper's Color Code is not to create an army of paranoid men who can't operate in life, but, rather, an opportunity for men to understand their environment and react accordingly.

READINESS

Should you find yourself in a dangerous situation (active shooter, emergency, natural disaster, etc.), how capable are you of protecting yourself and your loved ones? Do you have the physical and mental capacity to handle whatever life throws at you?

When asked about the famous Boy Scout motto "Be Prepared" and what a man should be prepared for, Lord Baden Powell answered, "Anything." It's difficult to fully understand and appreciate what dangerous situations you may find yourself in, which is why, now more than ever, it's imperative that you train your body and mind for whatever may come.

Physical fitness is a huge component of becoming a better protector. If, for example, you're fifty pounds overweight, do you honestly believe that you're fully capable of standing against evil or an emergency?

There was a time in my life when I actually weighed fifty pounds more than I do today. I stand at five feet ten and I weighed in at 235 pounds at my heaviest weight. I remember coming home from work one day and, as my kids pulled on my pant leg, begging me to jump on the trampoline, I had to look them in the eye and say, "I'm sorry guys, I can't jump on the trampoline." I could just as easily have said, "I'm sorry guys, I have voluntarily given up sovereignty over my body."

I could see the sadness in their eyes as I contemplated the pathetic situation I had created for myself.

If I couldn't jump on the trampoline with my children for a few minutes, I certainly couldn't outrun an active shooter, lift a car hood off my wife in an accident, or survive a fist fight with a would-be thief.

Just as physical health is critical, so is mental health. Do you have the mental fortitude, strength, and resiliency to deal with a violent or emergency situation? Can you keep your calm? Can you keep your wits about you? In the movie *Braveheart*, Malcolm Wallace responds to an angry and eager-to-fight young William Wallace, "I know you can fight but it's our wits that make us men."

Will you be the man on the news who rescues the children from an active shooter, or will you be the man who cowered in the corner because he was physically and mentally unprepared to handle himself in a difficult situation? Of course, the fear never goes away, but a man constantly strives to improve his body and mind to deal with a threat when it arises and the situation calls for it.

WEAPONS OF WAR

This is where I lose a lot of men. I want to be the first to tell you that I do not advocate unnecessary violence. Necessary? Yes. Unnecessary? No. Edmund Burke has stated, "The only thing necessary for the triumph of evil is for good men to do nothing."

It's a painful fact of life that, at some point, you may be required to stand up to violence. You don't go looking for it, but it may find you. When that day comes, you will want to have understood and trained with all the tools at your disposal in order to neutralize a threat.

Your body, for example, is a machine. As we've embraced the blindfold we've become accustomed to wearing and the ease of modernity, it is likely that machine has become like a rusted-over heap of metal. This is not how the body was intended to operate. A man's body was intended to work. Period. It's why we're bigger than women. It's why we're stronger than women. It's why we're faster than women. You are a workhorse.

Treat your body like it was intended to be treated in order to maximize its output. Exercise regularly. Fuel correctly. Rest properly. Train accordingly.

In addition to the care and maintenance of your body, spend time learning how to wield your body to do harm to another human being. Again, the goal is not to start trouble but to end it should it arise.

Secondary, but equally important, is learning how to use a firearm. Whether you believe in the second amendment or have a desire to own a gun is not relevant. The fact is that there are violent men who do, and they will use any tool they can against you and your loved ones.

With that said, you have to understand and, at least to some degree, know what the tools are, how they work, and how to operate them. If you aren't interested in owning a firearm, fine. But that does not mean you should not learn how to use one. Get firearm training. Go to a gun range. Learn that a firearm is only as dangerous as the man wielding it, and you'll see that guns are not the problem and, in many cases, may represent the solution.

These aren't easy conversations to have. I don't know many men who are interested in violence for the sake of being violent. I spent time overseas in a war zone. I've had countless conversations with elite military operators and law enforcement officers and not one of them wished for violence, but you can be damn sure all of them were prepared to do violence when called upon.

You can plead ignorance and hope it all works out, or you can prepare yourself for a day that hopefully never comes. Either way, understand that operating with your head in the sand is not the strategy of a Sovereign Men.

PROVISIONS

Any great leader of men knows that provisions quite literally spell the difference between a successful campaign and an unsuccessful one. We spend so much time acquiring trinkets and gizmos and gadgets that serve no real purpose in moving us toward our objectives but can't seem to wrap our heads around spending a little money, time, and attention on the provisions that could potentially save our lives.

Food storage, for example, has saved my bacon more than once. There was a time in my life (early in my marriage) when money was extremely tight. Each year, the youth of our community would sell bags of potatoes as a fundraiser. Every year my wife would buy a bag. There was one time in particular where my paycheck had been delayed by two weeks, and with no money in the bank account, we survived off potatoes for weeks. To this day, my wife continues to buy those bags of potatoes as well as other provisions we may need in times of struggle and emergency.

Speaking of emergencies, do you have adequate provisions in your home and car should you need to leave in a hurry? You might refer to this as a "bug-out bag" or "bolt bag." Having the tools and equipment needed to survive without food or power at the ready could possibly save your life.

I realize this is not an exhaustive list of the ways in which a man can be prepared to protect himself and his loved ones, but the goal is to get you thinking creatively about what skills, tools, and resources you may need to acquire in order to fulfill your responsibility to protect.

THE MINDSET—I AM A WARRIOR

I'll admit, I hate even using the word "warrior." It's extremely overused. I've heard it used to describe everything from artists to yoga practitioners to social media marketers. That said, it does paint an accurate picture of the mindset you need to incorporate in your life if you are to be the protector you are called to be.

Warriors train their bodies and minds. Warriors train with weapons. Warriors prepare their domains. If you are to be a Sovereign Man, you have to wrap your head around the notion that you are a modern-day warrior.

We, as men, have been asked to protect those who are incapable of protecting themselves as long as we've been on this planet. Sure, times have gotten easier, but there may come a day when you'll need to tap into your primal nature and do violence on behalf of yourself and others to protect those you love. Will you be adequately prepared for that day?

CHAPTER 5

PROVIDE

"A man who becomes conscious of the responsibility he bears toward a human being who affectionately waits for him, or to an unfinished work, will never be able to throw away his life. He knows the 'why' for his existence, and will be able to bear almost any 'how.'"
-Viktor Frankl

As long as we've been on this planet, it's been up to men to provide for their families and communities. Traditionally, this has been by way of physical provision, whether that means hunting for food to provide life-giving sustenance, or financially, to pay for the roof over our heads, the clothes on our backs, and the food in our bellies. Modern times have challenged the status quo as more and more women enter the workforce and more and more men choose to stay at home in what was traditionally the women's role in the family and society.

Let me be clear because there seems to be some misunderstanding when I bring up the word "provide." Does a man have a responsibility to provide for his family financially? At the end of the day, I believe that *is* his responsibility, but I also realize the dynamic of who brings home the bacon and who tends the house and children can vary from family to family. If something other than the traditional roles men and women play works for you and your household, more power to you.

That said, there is more than one way to provide, which I'll discuss in the following sections: Financial, Mental, Emotional, and Spiritual. A man's ability and capacity to master each of these areas represents the second point of his mission: provide.

FINANCIAL

Let's cover the financial topic because, as it stands today, the overwhelming majority of men still provide the financial support to the family (if this does not apply to your situation, I would still encourage you to read this section as it may become your responsibility in the future for any number of reasons: death, disability, layoff, and/or divorce).

There is a growing and disturbing trend that the number of welfare recipients is increasing, and the number of programs available is expanding. (More on this in Chapter 8.)

Let me be the first to say that I recognize there is a time and place for these programs, but I also recognize the fraud and blatant scandal that has ripped through these social welfare programs.

One of my stepfathers is a private investigator. He was hired by large corporations to investigate workers' compensation fraud. He would routinely come home and show me surveillance videos of "injured" men fraudulently collecting workers' compensation. There were men who had, for example, "broken their backs," yet found the time, energy, and physical strength to mow the lawn, do some chores around the house, go on shopping sprees to the mall, and many other activities.

Now, I realize this one particular example may not be a social welfare issue, rather an insurance issue, but it illustrates the way one man can take advantage of the system in order to live inconsistently with the way he was meant to live.

Although I do not agree with any many who fraudulently mooches off any other working man, I can certainly see the appeal. After all, what sounds better than collecting a paycheck while sitting in your basement playing video games and watching *All My Children*, infomercials, and *The Price Is Right* (or whatever shows air during the day)?

But as nice as that may sound, the reality is that a man's desire to get something for nothing is at direct odds with his sovereignty. Programs change or go away altogether, the money runs out, and/or you get caught. A man must resist the urge to get something for nothing. There is nothing more damaging to the heart and mind of a man than knowing he is not providing for himself and those who rely on him.

I remember times in my life where my wife and I were living on credit to make ends meet. We were robbing Peter to pay Paul. Those were some of the most stressful times in my life and times I wish never to experience again.

On the other side, we've had times of extreme financial abundance in our family. There is nothing so satisfying as coming home from a long week of work knowing that, although you're tired, your family and loved ones are benefitting from the results of your labors.

To provide financially is the work of men. Unfortunately, there seems to be some confusion about our relationship with money. Money is simply a metric of perceived value. It's not the *only* metric, but it's *a* metric. When a man goes to work, his employer pays him based on the value he will provide to the company. When a client hires an advisor, that client is paying based on the perceived value he will receive. This is why it feels so good to make money. It's not necessarily the money itself; it's the value a man brings to the marketplace. If there's one thing we want in this life, it's to be valued.

MENTAL

Outside of the financial provisions, a man must also learn to provide mentally for himself and his family. A man's ability to develop the mental fortitude and resilience to lead in times of feast and famine is of utmost importance.

Let's face it, life is tough. Life can be a challenge. You and your family are likely to run into any number of problems that could derail the plans you have set for yourself: disability, injury, lawsuit, death, divorce, bankruptcy. Without the mental fortitude to plan for and overcome the events you are likely to experience in your lifetime, you and your family could find yourself in ruin.

There have been times in my marriage when all seemed lost. Mortgage payments went unpaid. Tempers flared. Anger and resentment welled up. It's times like these that people will turn to the man for mental guidance and support. Will you break down when all seems lost, or will you step up to the challenge. One will never truly know until that day comes, but if you do have a desire to lead your family effectively, mental provision, fortitude, and resilience are musts.

What knowledge have you acquired? What experiences can you draw upon? What is your ability to effectively articulate the vision you wish to cast? These are all ways in which a man provides mental clarity and strength as the head of his house, his business, and his community.

EMOTIONAL

When I talk about masculinity, the last thing most men would think about is emotion. The lie we've been fed that men are not emotional just isn't reality.

Think about the last time you felt something. Pride in your son for scoring the game-winning touchdown. Fear that you weren't going to be able make a payment on time. Sorrow as you thought about the fight you and your wife got into last night. Emotions are something we all experience. Rather than run from those emotions, a man should strive to understand and regulate them.

Unfortunately, most men operate at the mercy of their emotions.

As a coach to my children's sports teams for the last four years, I can tell you that I've seen some horrendous behavior on the field by men whom I would otherwise completely respect. I've been guilty of those emotional outbursts as well.

But tell me, how does suppressing your emotions at the risk of blowing up at some unknowable future date add to your ability to live in sovereignty? What if, instead, you choose not to suppress your emotions but rather to understand them? And, just as valuable, understand the emotions of those closest to you.

Emotional intelligence is a cornerstone of masculinity. If a man can understand *why* he feels the way he does, does that not arm him with the ability to do something about it?

After all, if sovereignty is the objective, any tool that allows us to achieve more is of the utmost importance.

People are going to be sad. People are going to get mad. People are going to feel offended and hurt. You will experience these emotions as well. It's okay. It's part of being human. The more you can understand the emotions in yourself and the emotions in others, the better you are able to adjust the way in which you approach any number of challenging scenarios.

You are a rock—the rock that many will look to in times of struggle, fear, and sorrow. That does not mean you aren't allowed to display emotions; it means that you need to use those emotions as a display of love, guidance, and direction to those who look to you. The less we try to eliminate our emotions and the more we start to decipher and decode what it is they're trying to tell us, the more likely we are to be driven toward action that serves us and others.

SPIRITUAL ———————————————————————————————————

Whether you're Christian, Catholic, Muslim, Hindu, or Buddhist, I think we can all agree that there is some unknown, unseen force that is greater than the dimension in which we live.

It is my belief that, unless we learn to tap into this higher power, we severely limit ourselves on the inputs available to live life as a Sovereign Man. Call it your conscious, your intuition, your gut, Jiminy Cricket, the universe, God, the Holy Ghost, the Holy Spirit, or a combination of them all, this extra sense has the ability to warn you of impending danger and illuminate a successful path.

Most of us, however, live life too full to recognize this power. Think about it. When is the last time you took a break? When did you last have time for any level of reflection in your day-to-day activities? When's the last time you really thought about how your time is meant to be spent? Tell me, where in your day do you have the time and margin to tap into this higher power that will allow you to escape the rat race you so desperately want to escape?

More than likely, the answer is that there is no time for that. You're always in "go mode." So, you continue to live the same way, day in and day out for the rest of your life.

If we have any hope of tapping into this higher power (regardless of what you choose to call it), we must create space for ourselves to listen, to feel, to hear, and to see.

In early 2005, I found myself walking into the dusty building in the middle of a compound that was once an Iraqi detention facility. It was my first day on the job, and to say most of what ensued in the following months is all a bit of a haze would be a massive understatement.

I already mentioned the fourteen soldiers who lost their lives who were represented on the entry wall of that building. But what I did not mention was that, when we returned from our tour, we learned that the unit replacing us had lost ten soldiers in the first week they were there. A suicide bomber drove a truck to the front gate, maneuvered through the barriers, and detonated his explosive vehicle, killing ten soldiers guarding the gate to the base.

With the loss of life from the unit before us and the unit that replaced us, how was it possible that our unit did not suffer a single loss? What was the difference? What separated us from the unit before and after?

We prayed as a unit morning, noon, and night. Our families prayed for us back home. We read scriptures together, and we lived our lives and carried out our duties in accordance with the guidance we received from that Higher Power.

The fact that I can't clearly articulate the difference or prove beyond a shadow of doubt the existence of such a power seems to be a problem for many men.

We tend to believe that if we can't physically feel it or see it, it must not exist. Instead, we choose to lean only on what we can prove. In addition to that, many men feel like tapping into a higher power makes them subservient to that power.

Prayer, meditation, divine guidance, and scripture study, however, do not make you subservient to those things, but rather give you the ability to tap into a power far greater and more powerful than we can understand. That does not weaken your independence; it only strengthens it.

THE MINDSET—I AM A SOURCE OF CREATION, RESOURCES, AND PROVISION

Men provide. Period. We are useful. We bring ideas, thoughts, inspiration, and knowledge to the table. If we aren't willing or capable of doing so, what good is it having us around?

Now, some people will hear that and think it's too harsh or doesn't accurately reflect our value in this world. Wrong. Our value in this world is in direct proportion to the value we provide and create. It's what we do. Think about your tendency to offer solutions and solve problems, even when unsolicited. If that doesn't highlight our natural desire to improve our station and the station of those we care about, I don't know what does.

Sovereign Men don't mind that others rely on us for provision, either. Some may think that if the man is the sole or weighted provider of all that is required to sustain a family, business, or community's way of life, it's somehow unfair. But it's not unfair at all. It's not unfair because we too gain from this arrangement. We gain the sense of pride, satisfaction, and fulfillment that comes from looking at our tribes and knowing they're thriving in large part due to us.

I've known men who have been laid off for any number of reasons. It's damaging to a man's psyche. I can see it in his eyes. It's written on his face. I can sense it in his demeanor. When a man is incapable of providing all that's necessary to lead, he loses his sense of purpose and direction and, as a result, the battle for his heart and mind.

I've been there. I've been in situations in my life where I knew I was doing and providing less than I was capable of. It's the most demoralizing experience in the world. Being fully capable of providing and producing results in my life, on the other hand, is the most rewarding feeling a man can experience. There's nothing more liberating to the heart and mind of a man than knowing he is enough as evidence of what he alone has created.

CHAPTER 6

PRESIDE

"Leadership is not just one quality, but rather a blend of many qualities; and while no one individual possesses all of the needed talents that go into leadership, each man can develop a combination to make him a leader."
-Vince Lombardi

The third point of a Sovereign Man's mission is to preside. This is the one that tends to generate the most confusion. To clarify, presiding is about leading those you have an obligation and responsibility to lead, including yourself.

Your ability to lead effectively in every area of your life is a huge part of what makes you a man. Take the family unit, for example. As a father, I recognize the noble calling of raising little humans. My sons and daughter look to me as a source of guidance, direction, and inspiration. If I cannot or will not lead them, what right do I have to the title of father?

But one doesn't have to be a father in order to lead. There are plenty of other opportunities to lead in your life. If you run a business, you're a leader. If you're a coach, you're a leader. If you've been tasked with even the most menial of projects at work, you're a leader. And the same holds true in these scenarios: if you cannot or will not lead those looking to you, what right do you have to the title you carry?

Even more important than leading others is the ability to effectively lead yourself. My friend Andy Frisella, with The MFCEO Project, has talked numerous times about his followers' desire to "be their own boss." What Andy says is that, whether you own a business or you're an employee, you *already* are your own boss.

That couldn't be more true. If you refuse to look at yourself as the ultimate authority in your life, you have no business working toward your own sovereignty. Every day you'll be faced with a thousand decisions to make. No one else is going to make these decisions for you. There is only *you*.

Unfortunately, what I see in many men is an unhealthy desire to sit the fence. What they are waiting for, I really don't know. Maybe they're waiting for permission to make a decision. That makes sense. We've been conditioned since childhood to ask permission before acting. When I was little, my mom would make us recite the phrase, "May I please be excused?" before we stepped away from the dinner table. While I can understand the need for structure, I can't help but wonder if this is just one of the many ways we've been programmed to sit and wait for authorization to carry out an action.

Truth be told, most men are scared to lead themselves, let alone others. They know that if they mess up, they'll be mocked, ridiculed, chastised, and even punished for making the wrong choice. Rather than expose themselves to the consequences of messing up, they don't take action. As Aristotle would say, "In order to avoid criticism, do nothing, say nothing, be nothing."

What these men fail to see is that by finally making a choice, they are, potentially for the first time in their lives, giving themselves a fighting chance. And getting yourself in the game is the first step to masculine leadership.

LEADERS GO FIRST

A leader is incapable of effectively leading if he isn't willing to do the very thing he has asked those following him to do. Leaders always go first. Period.

For example, there were men in my National Guard unit I would follow to hell and back because I recognized experience in them. I had seen that they had done the very thing they were asking me to do. They knew the pitfalls. They knew where to step. They knew which way to go. They had the map.

But there were others I wouldn't trust with anything, let alone my life. By their very nature and their inability to lead from the front, they undermined their ability to effectively carry out a mission. So it goes with sovereignty. I cannot teach others to reclaim their sovereignty if I have not done it for myself. It's disingenuous at best and a blatant lie at worst.

Don't fret. If going first is something you're not used to, there are ways to develop the desire and ability to lead from the front. We're going to talk about this a lot as we get into Part III: The Code of Conduct, but for now, just know that everything begins with practice.

The process of going first requires you to *actually* go first. There is nothing I can share with you here that will replace the courage and the subsequent action required to take a step into the unknown. It's something that *has* to be experienced.

And what an experience it is. If you're a man who's never had to make decisions on his own or never had to live with the consequence of those decisions, this is a liberating feeling and the first step to presiding on every front of your life.

The notion of going first and making decisions is so critical to becoming a Sovereign Man that I've already started teaching my sons the principle of going first and making their own decisions. Just the other day, we were out hiking in the mountains of southern

Utah. I was on point with my sons in tow when I remembered the principle of leaders go first. I asked my oldest son (he's nine) to take the lead. He did without hesitation until we reached a fork in the trail.

"Dad, which trail should I take?" he asked.

"I don't know," I answered, "you're leading today." As it turns out, he took the wrong trail. We walked for about a half mile and hit a dead end.

"Dad, what should we do?"

"I don't know," I answered again, "you're leading today."

He turned us around and got us on the right trail.

I understand it can be risky to make big decisions. I realize there's more on the line than traveling half a mile in the wrong direction. But the principle remains: leaders go first. If you have any hope of presiding effectively, you're going to have to make the first move.

WITHOUT A FOLLOWER, THERE IS NO LEADER

An effective leader is able to make the first move *and* he is able to cast a vision. Without vision, there will be no one to lead, and without anyone to lead, there is no leader.

If you, as a father, husband, coach, employer, product manager, et cetera, don't have a vision for the future and the ability to clearly articulate that vision, you have no chance of leading others. Unfortunately, most men don't know what they want out of life and therefore are missing the third component of the trifecta that is the mission to protect, provide, and preside.

What a shame, considering the world is craving masculine leadership more than it ever has. On every level, men are failing to effectively lead those who would gladly follow if only they had someone to carry the torch.

Again, I refer to *Braveheart.* In a scene where William Wallace and Robert the Bruce discuss the risk to the noblemen of Scotland in fighting for their freedom, William Wallace says, "Now tell me, what does it mean to be noble? Your title gives you claim to the throne of our country, but men don't follow titles, they follow courage. Now, our people know you. Noble and common, they respect you. And if you would just *lead* them to freedom they'd follow you. And, so would I."

People are hungry for leadership. They want direction. They want guidance. They want a sense of purpose and belonging. They want a battle to fight. You, as a man, can be the flag bearer of that battle if only you choose to be.

The notion that you can lead others into a battle of your choosing is intoxicating. Yes, you will have a burden to bear. There will be those who do not believe in you or the battle you're engaged in. You'll be met with your fair share of critics, but I cannot think of a more exciting life to live than one where you're anxiously engaged in a noble pursuit, standing shoulder to shoulder with those who believe in you and your cause.

If you truly want to lead, you must know your battle and cast the vision. Only then, when you've proven yourself worthy, will others follow you.

LEADERS CREATE LEADERS

A leader's singular purpose should be to create additional leaders, who will carry the battle forward or leave to lead their own battles. Too many men believe that a leader creates followers indefinitely.

Consider the boss who refuses to teach his subordinates all he knows out of fear the subordinates will one day replace him and/or steal his business. These men aren't leaders; they're managers, at best. Managing people as opposed to leading people does nothing to enhance the mission, and it makes people dependent on as opposed to independent of you, the so-called leader. It strips away sovereignty.

A genuine leader understands and maintains an abundance mentality. That is to say, he knows there is more than enough to go around and does not concern himself with what a subordinate may go out and create on his own. He takes pride in knowing that, one day, those he leads will surpass all he has accomplished himself. This does not intimidate the Sovereign Man, but rather, it fills him with joy, fulfillment, and satisfaction.

As valuable as it is for others to be effectively led, it is also advantageous to the leader himself. If, for example, I refuse to share *all* my knowledge and expertise and instead withhold what could give others the power to act independently of me, I have enslaved myself and become a prisoner of that knowledge.

In the military, we called this decentralized command. I cannot possibly leverage my time, talents, and knowledge as well as others' without giving them the authority to make decisions without my approval.

I am experiencing this in my business now. I made a goal in early 2017 to take my family on a Hawaiian vacation. Fortunately, through a little planning and a lot of hard work, we are able to turn this into a reality. If I do not adequately prepare my team to handle all the decisions that go into running a successful business on a day-to-day basis, there is no possible way for me to step away for something I've worked so hard to enjoy.

The objective of a leader is to develop new leaders. We, as men, have a moral obligation to teach all we know. There will come a day when we ask our sons to lead their tribes. Doing all you can to equip them for that day is a genuine mark of a Sovereign Man.

THE MINDSET—I LEAD MYSELF AND THOSE I HAVE AN OBLIGATION TO LEAD

There is a debate that calls into question whether leaders are born or made. I believe there are those who are born with the capacity to lead more effectively than some, but I do not discount man's ability to develop the skills required to lead others.

Although it may be more challenging for some, it is simply a matter of choice. Do you want to be leading the charge or do you want to be following? The reality is that it's probably a combination of both. I don't consider myself a leader in every scenario. There are plenty of opportunities for me to follow. And there are more than enough opportunities for us, as men, to step into the calling to preside.

You have been wired to find a battle that calls to you, to rally the troops, and to engage. Knowing that it's your calling to lead does not make it any easier; it simply means that you are fully capable of doing so. Right now, your ability to lead others is untapped potential.

The first step in unlocking that potential is making the decision to do so and recognizing the need to lead yourself as the man you are fully capable of becoming. A Sovereign Man realizes that leading himself is what makes him sovereign in the first place. He fully honors that opportunity and obligation by helping those in his care do the same.

PART III

THE CODE OF
CONDUCT

*"In matters of style, swim with the current; in matters of principle,
stand like a rock."*
-Thomas Jefferson

Every great society and every great movement agrees to adhere to a
set of rules and a set of guidelines, a Code of Conduct if you will.

Romans adhered to *Romanitas* or *mos maiorum*, which means
"the custom of the ancestors." Although this code was unwritten,
these models, practices, and traditions shaped much of Roman
behavior.

Among the personal virtues Romans aspired to live up to were
mercy, dignity, tenacity, frugality, industriousness, and truthful-
ness. Among the public virtues Romans strived to adhere to were
abundance, equity, prosperity, confidence, justice, and freedom.

Dating back even further (1754 B.C.), we find the Code of Ham-
murabi from the ancient Babylonian people. This code of 282 laws

can be found on seven-and-a-half-feet-tall stone monuments and covers everything from slander to trade to slavery and theft to the duties of workers and divorce.

Christians adhere to the Ten Commandments. Members of the medical community swear to uphold the Hippocratic Oath.

Warriors of every nation and every time period have all lived up to a code, from the Spartan army's code of honor and discipline to medieval knights' code of chivalry to the Japanese samurai's Bushido or "Way of the Warrior."

When I joined the military, I was expected to memorize the Code of the United States Fighting Force, which illustrated the way we, as soldiers, were to conduct ourselves on the battlefield and in captivity.

Even pirates adhered to a code, which came to be known as the Articles of Agreement. The pirates' Articles of Agreement covered everything from discipline to division of stolen items to desertion to the hierarchy of the ship's command and crew.

Too many men live their lives without a personal Code of Conduct for the way they will conduct themselves in any given situation and in any given environment. Consider, for example, the man who steps out on his wife. In hindsight and after the excitement has died down, he will justify his actions because he "temporarily lost himself." He forgot who he was. He let the heat of the moment get to him.

I've heard men balk at the notion of a Code of Conduct. Many men believe the idea that living up to a set of self-imposed guidelines somehow places unnecessary restrictions on them. On the surface, this makes sense. Rules, regulations, and guidelines are, by definition, restrictive.

But I'd have you consider that the healthy, constructive guidelines we establish enable us to live fuller, richer lives than living free from the "burden" of these limitations does.

Take, for example, the man who decides to consume whatever food, drinks, and substances he feels so inclined to consume in any given moment. Does this man not increase the chance of developing a crippling medical condition, decreasing his standard of living, and/or shortening his years? Which is worse, imposing a set of standards on yourself or suffering the consequence of doing whatever the hell you feel like?

In Part III, we break down the Sovereign Man's Code of Conduct. We looked at the "what" in Part II: The Mission. Now we're going to uncover the "how."

It is through the thirteen virtues we highlight that you maximize your ability to live a sovereign life and effectively carry out your mission to protect, provide, and preside. In addition to the Code we cover, you will also learn the mindset required to master each virtue. And, where most books end with information, we encourage you to use this section as a field manual for your day-to-day operations. For this reason, we've also included a set of skills that you will be challenged to engage in on your journey to become the master of your heart and mind.

My journey from rock bottom to what has become the best days of my life has been a long, slow process. I've had my share of ups and downs along the way. These thirteen virtues have been my guiding compass to keep me on the narrow path of the Sovereign Man.

CHAPTER 7

SELF-RELIANCE

"Men are anxious to improve their circumstances, but are unwilling to improve themselves; therefore they remain bound."
-James Allen

At the root of the sovereign virtues lies the desire and ability of a man to be completely self-reliant, free from the burden of dependence on anyone or anything. Please do not misunderstand me: in no way, shape, or form does this mean that a man cannot or should not request and/or accept help. It simply means that a Sovereign Man strives to help himself first before relying on the help of others.

Unfortunately, much of society seems to believe it cannot operate without the help and assistance of others. Self-reliance seems to be a dying virtue.

Whether we're referring to government assistance for companies that are "too big to fail," access to supplemented and free health insurance, or the staggering rate of consumption of welfare programs, the number of men capitalizing on these handouts is outrageously high. According to the United States Department of Agriculture, the United States has spent nearly $75,000,000,000 in food-related welfare alone through June 2017.

Which begs the question, why?

The idea of dependence on others isn't a difficult concept to wrap our heads around. The simple answer is that it's easier. It's always easier to live off another man's efforts than it is to live off our own.

When notorious bank robber Willie Sutton was asked by a reporter why he stole from banks, he answered, "Because that's where the money is." Well, that's part of the answer. The part he left out was that's where the *easy* money is. During his forty-year criminal career, Sutton is said to have stolen an estimated $30,000,000 in today's currency.

But easier doesn't always equal better. Every time a man unjustly profits off the work of another man, a piece of his soul dies—unless he's a sociopath. We've all been there. When I was younger, I stole a pack of baseball cards from the convenience store. It ate at me so much that I went back, bought another pack of cards, and "accidentally" forgot to grab my change before rushing out of the store.

The feelings of guilt, remorse, and shame that stem from stealing from another man don't go away as we develop from boys to men. The man who knows full well he's capable of providing for himself yet chooses not to can hardly bear to look at himself in the mirror, let alone confidently lock eyes with another man.

Shame is just one way in which the damaging effects of dependence manifest themselves and rot the heart and mind of a man. Some men get angry, some withdraw, some even become violent. But the underlying consequence is always the same, as a sense of depression clouds the judgment of an otherwise moral man.

CULTURE OF VICTIMHOOD

Less devious but equally damaging to the condition of man is the idea that somehow he is a victim of his environment and/or others. Barring severe physical limitations or mental handicap, every man is capable of paving his own way.

In the fall of 2016, I was invited to participate in the Spartan Agoge, a grueling sixty-hour endurance event in the mountains of Vermont. I spent two and a half days with roughly 120 other men and women, in my own blood, sweat, and tears. There were several moments on that mountain when I almost threw in the towel, where I almost gave up on myself and quit.

One instance in particular was during an extremely difficult hike up a series of mountain ridges called "Blood Route" (a fitting name). I was feeling particularly sorry for myself that afternoon as my knees seemed to grind with every agonizing step. By this time, the sores on my feet had ripped wide open, and pain blazed through my lower back and right hip every time I set my right foot down.

During the pity party I happened to be throwing for myself, I looked over to catch a glimpse of another team. This team comprised veteran athletes. But these athletes weren't just veterans— they were all amputees. Some were missing arms or legs, yet here they were, not only participating in one of the most demanding challenges I'd ever found myself in, but smiling. They were working together. They were actually enjoying themselves.

We are not victims unless we choose to be. The world is not conspiring against us. No one is out to get us. This understanding is what gives us the power to do more than we believe we are capable of.

Our parents, teachers, coaches, and much of society has spent a lot of time telling us it's okay to do just enough and that the lack of results we've been experiencing in life is the result of what someone or something else has done to us.

If you are to gain your Sovereignty, you must reject the idea that you are a victim. Look, I get it, you may have been dealt a bad hand. Someone may have actually done something to you. But there comes a time when your excuses expire, and all that is left is what you've done or failed to do with the cards you've been asked to play.

You are capable of so much more than you currently think you are. The only way you're going to learn that lesson is to stop asking for so much help and stop placing blame where it doesn't belong. Take a look at children. You don't see a child who is learning to walk wallow in self-pity when he falls. He simply gets back up and tries again. Many times, he'll ignore or swat away the hand that's extended to help. In many ways, the child is attempting to answer the question John Eldredge, author of *Wild at Heart*, says all men are attempting to answer: "Am I enough and do I have what it takes?"

Do you? There's only one way to find out.

BEHOLDEN TO NO ONE

What I've come to realize is that the more we play the victim card and the more we ask for something we have not yet earned, the more we find ourselves at the mercy of other people, organizations, and even our governments.

In 2007, I became a financial advisor. As I learned the ropes, educated myself on the products and solutions I would be offering to my clients, and built my financial planning practice, I found myself gravitating toward working with business owners, especially in the medical field. Up until this point, I had been working with individuals who were mostly employees of organizations as opposed to the owners of them.

As I immersed myself in the plans I would be offering my business clients, I came across the frequently used term "golden handcuffs." This term is used to describe employee benefits (typically retirement plans) offered by employers to discourage employees from leaving the company and working elsewhere.

Therein lies the problem. Although golden handcuffs may not seem like a bad idea (there is an actual benefit being offered), the concept illustrates perfectly the motive of parties to offer the benefits in the first place: to limit your freedom, your options, and your sovereignty.

I have firsthand experience with a company who tried to limit the options available to me. I spent nearly six years with a previous financial planning firm. We had a great working relationship. They provided the training and support. I provided the revenue through clients and services. Pretty good deal, right? Yeah, it was great, until it wasn't.

After six years with the firm, I started to dig into the numbers. By this time, I had outgrown the limited training they were offering. Outside of the office they paid for and the administrative support they provided, there were no other benefits to the partnership. In fact, in digging through the numbers, I came to the conclusion that the benefits being offered equaled roughly $2,500 per month. That sounded great, until I realized the commission I was giving the company through my clients was roughly $4,000 per month.

At that moment, I knew I had to make a decision to start my own financial planning firm. Long story short, I approached the firm I had been working with to inform them I would be leaving, to which they responded by informing me that, six years earlier, I had signed a contract that stipulated that my clients were not really my clients, but theirs. If I were to leave, I'd be leaving roughly $70,000 of residual income on the table.

That was a difficult decision to make but, ultimately, one I proceeded with anyway. That said, I know for a fact the fear of losing that residual income has kept plenty of advisors exactly where they currently are—unhappy, dissatisfied, and resentful, but $70,000 a year richer.

As I debated whether to leave or stay, I could not ignore the words that echoed in my head from a coach I had hired to help me grow my financial planning practice.

When he left his former financial planning firm, he had a very similar experience. He marched into his boss's office to inform him of his resignation. His boss responded by stating, "Mark, you'll never be able to make it on your own. It's too hard, it's too challenging, and you can't do it without us. You'll be back."

With all the courage and gusto he could muster, he retorted, "I'd rather live in a cardboard box than be your bitch the rest of my life," and marched out of the office.

Mark now owns a financial planning firm that manages over $7.5 billion in assets.

COGNITIVE DISTORTIONS

At the end of the day, I believe it is nothing more than fear that keeps us from relying on the fruits of our own efforts. It's fear of the unknown. It's fear of uncertainty. It's fear that somehow things will go horribly wrong. For this reason, we cling to our lifelines to avoid being drowned in the sea of negative consequences we may find ourselves in.

The problem is magnified by defense mechanisms we, as humans, have relied upon for thousands of years. They're called cognitive distortions. These distortions of reality are designed to keep us safe, but at the end of the day, they're lies and delusional thoughts about how bad the situation really may be.

I understand how destructive these distortions can be. During the darkest time in my life—my separation from my wife—I would often sit alone with my thoughts in the evening (by the way, I don't recommend doing that). I would think about what went wrong in our marriage and how I could fix it. More often than not, I would jump to the worst possible outcome or think that the world was somehow going to end because of our separation.

"She's going to ask for a divorce any minute."

"She's going to take my son away."

"My son will grow up thinking I didn't love him."

"I'll turn out just like my dad."

"My life will be over."

I tortured myself through a series of distortions that had little basis in reality. We do this so we can take action on improving ourselves or remove ourselves from the danger we may face.

The problem is that it might actually work. Our lies may keep us safe, secure, comfortable . . . and mediocre. But is that really any way to live?

John A. Shedd said, "A ship in harbor is safe, but that is not what ships are built for." You're not built for mediocrity. You're built to do something more. That something more requires you to shut your mind off and face the fear you may have always been too weak to stand against.

One of my close friends and original members of the Iron Council, Joe Kasprzak, uses the question, "What's the worst that could happen?" An objective look at the answer typically reveals that the potential reward is well worth the perceived risk.

THE MINDSET—NO ONE OWES ME A THING

One of the most damaging beliefs a man can adhere to is that somehow someone owes him something—that his boss owes him a job, that his wife owes him her affection, that the government owes him health insurance. It just isn't true. No one owes you anything.

The sooner you realize that, the sooner you release yourself from the dependence of others to provide the necessities and comforts of life. Most men can't handle this realization; therefore, they play the game of life in a way that is inconsistent with the way they were meant to live it: big.

When we live by the notion that people owe us something, we cripple ourselves and our ability to live life on our terms. It reminds me of the agencies that rescue wounded animals. Many times, rescued animals cannot be returned to the wild because they've become too dependent, despite the efforts of the rescuers, on the provisions that no longer have to be earned.

You too belong in the wild. And when you become accustomed to having all your needs met by others, you hinder your ability to live as a Sovereign Man. The truth is there is no one here to rescue you from all that you're going to face. But that's okay; you don't need them to. In his poem "Invictus," William Ernest Henley (*Book of Verses*, 1888) captures the notion that we are already enough and have within ourselves all that is needed to be free:

Out of the night that covers me,
Black as the pit from pole to pole,
I thank whatever gods may be
For my unconquerable soul.

In the fell clutch of circumstance
I have not winced nor cried aloud.
Under the bludgeonings of chance
My head is bloody, but unbowed.

Beyond this place of wrath and tears
Looms but the Horror of the shade,
And yet the menace of the years
Finds and shall find me unafraid.

It matters not how strait the gate,
How charged with punishments the scroll,
I am the master of my fate,
I am the captain of my soul.

The only way to survive and thrive is to sever the ties that keep you domesticated and weak—to be your own man and to recognize that you already have all that you need. In other words, to be the master of your fate and the captain of your soul.

THE SKILL SET

Cut the Cord. Take a look at your life and inventory where you are relying upon other people to provide the tools, skills, resources, and provisions you should be providing for yourself. Then, sever them.

Who are you overly dependent on for emotional support? Is anyone giving you money or resources that shouldn't be? Do you have other people's tools, equipment, or belongings? What comforts are you enjoying that you didn't earn? Have you taken something that does not belong to you?

This is going to be extremely difficult because you've become accustomed to living with something you didn't have to earn for yourself. Naturally this is going to be hard until you build up the mental, emotional, and physical capacity to provide for yourself in these areas. Deal with it. It's going to be tough. It's going to be uncomfortable. It's going to be awkward. But it's only temporary.

Soon, you'll build up the mental fortitude, emotional resiliency, and physical strength to deal with all that life has to offer, and you'll wonder what took you so long to stand on your own two feet.

Find a Way or Make One. Years ago, I was responsible for the twelve- to fourteen-year-olds' Scouting program in my neighborhood. One of the requirements for the boys each year was to participate in what was called a High Adventure. For our High Adventure, the boys chose a two-day seventeen-mile hike in the mountains of southern Utah.

Before we left, I asked the boys to come up with a motto for their adventure. They adopted the Latin motto, *Inveniam viam aut faciam*, which means, "I will find a way or make one."

During the most grueling sections of the hike, the boys would spur each other on with their motto, *Inveniam viam aut faciam*. We successfully completed the hike with no major hiccups, but now, even four years later, the boys (who are now young men) remind me of that motto as a remembrance to overcome the most difficult challenges they face on their own two feet.

There's no way around it: you are going to face challenges and hardships. There will be obstacles that stand in your path. You can allow those obstacles to deter you. You can tuck tail and retreat to the life you've always lived, or you can decide right now that you will not quit and that the only way for you to go is forward.

Too many men give up too early. Too many men let the slightest hurdle scare them away from what they say they want most. Don't be that type of man. Live knowing that, when all seems lost, you always have the ability to find a way or make one.

CHAPTER 8

INTENTIONALITY

"The only person you are destined to become is the person you decide to be."
-Ralph Waldo Emerson

Take a look around society today and you're likely to see the equivalent of millions of mindless, soulless robots wandering through our streets. For years and years, we've been conditioned by our parents, spouses, children, employers, mainstream media, and the government to behave a certain way and to carry out a set of predetermined duties without asking too many questions.

More specifically, take a look at your day and ask yourself honestly if your life is a series of deliberate and intentional decisions or if it's simply a series of patterns and habits you've developed over a lifetime of carrying out orders. Let me illustrate by detailing the average man's day.

The average man wakes up, hits the snooze button a couple of times, and gives himself just enough time to grab a shower, brush his teeth, and change into the same clothes he wears every day. He jumps into his car and sits in traffic for an hour or longer (he'll typically listen to the same music or podcasts he always does) to get to a job where a stack of papers and projects awaits his arrival. If he's lucky he'll live up to his boss's expectations and be awarded

with the opportunity to take a quick lunch
back to the office, where he continues the ι
out, sits in some more traffic, gets home, ki
grabs some dinner, tucks the kids into bed, w
of his go-to TV show, hits the sack, and wake,
again—every day for the rest of his life.

Please do not misunderstand me. Developing l　　　　.ᴜ ns
is a healthy practice. In fact, the mind is consι ..ιy looking to
develop these patterns in order to preserve energy and enhance its
capacity to do more when it counts. These routines and patterns
(such as brushing your teeth) are the very systems that allow you to
focus on much more productive and meaningful work.

But how many habits can you identify that produce anything but
efficiency and effectiveness? Take the action of hitting the snooze
button from my example above. For whatever reason, the man who
continually hits snooze has told himself a narrative long enough
that he actually starts to believe his own bullshit. Perhaps he tells
himself that he deserves more sleep, or that getting fifteen more
minutes of sleep is a healthy decision, or he's convinced himself
that those few more minutes of sleep will ensure he's more productive throughout his day.

Even worse than believing the stories he tells himself, it isn't
long before he no longer needs to believe it—it's actually hard-
wired into his brain. No more thinking. No more processing. Just
executing the orders the electrons in his brain have requested.

THE MERCY OF OTHERS

As with any battle, knowing the enemy is crucial. If we are to
reclaim and maintain our sovereignty, we must know what we're
up against. I want to be very clear, I don't believe the world is out
to get us. I don't subscribe to the notion of "haters." But one thing
I have recognized is that, at times, people's interests are at direct
odds with mine.

erstanding and accepting this for what it is puts you in a
sition of power and control. If, for example, my six-year-old son
wants to stay up until midnight every night, I know that is at direct
odds with my objective as a father to raise healthy, balanced children. He's going to use every tactic he can to get what he wants.
Do I believe that makes him bad or the enemy or a "hater?" No, it
just means he's looking out for himself. I, as a Sovereign Man, can
understand that.

More devious is the competitor who may have just opened his
office across town. It may not be enough for him to open his doors
and conduct himself with honor and integrity. He may decide to
spread malicious rumors about your business conduct. He may
even attempt to reach out to your existing customers and falsify
your business dealings or bring into play your moral, ethical, and
legal integrity. At this point, you have a choice to make. Do you get
dragged into the dirt and play at his level (which would only help
prove his claims), or do you take the ethical high ground and stay
above the garbage he would otherwise drag you into?

Understanding and accepting that there are those who want to
control you really isn't that difficult when your head is clear. It's
when the choices, actions, and words of others have negatively
impacted you that it becomes a challenge. The emotions that creep
up when this happens are the biggest threat to your ability to keep
a clear head and position yourself to maximize choices.

When I was in seventh grade, I allowed another kid to occupy
space in my mind. I allowed my emotions to take over and did the
only thing I could think of at the time: fight him. Looking back
now, I don't remember what the fight was about, but I do remember
the consequence. I was suspended and was very close to being sent
to another school. It may sound like schoolyard antics from a boy
who was still wet behind the ears, but I'd be willing to bet you've
seen grown men (and perhaps yourself) engage in the very same
behavior.

Rash, emotional decisions based on the actions of others cloud our judgment, cause us to do stupid things, limit the choices we have, and keep us from making intentional decisions in our lives.

Do not allow others to occupy real estate in your mind. Understand that most people are out to serve themselves. Very rarely do they care about you. You might be an easy stepping-stone to what they want and, therefore, find yourself as collateral damage. Strive to understand people's motives, keep calm, use your head, regulate your emotions, and maintain your choices.

THE MERCY OF OURSELVES

The far greater threat to our ability to make choices than the child who just wants to stay up late or the competitor who wants to steal our business is our ability get in our own way.

We aren't just at the mercy of others; we are at the mercy of ourselves. More specifically, we are at the mercy of our choices, or lack thereof.

Make no mistake. Everything in life is a choice, whether you decide to acknowledge that or not. Most men do not. What may have started out as a choice became a pattern, and, as it goes, what became a pattern has now become a rut.

It's in our nature to look for the easy path. Staying in the rut will always be easier than carving a new one. So, rather than choose to consume new information, we continue to do the same things over and over and over again because it's easier.

This is how we sabotage ourselves. What may have worked for us in the past will no longer work for us moving forward. Priorities may have changed. You may have hit a plateau and are no longer experiencing the compounding gains you once enjoyed.

I know this is certainly true of me as I began my health journey four years ago. Losing the first thirty pounds was relatively easy; the next ten, moderate; and the last ten has fluctuated. I began to grow stagnant because I refused to expand the information I consumed. I stopped hitting personal records, I stopped losing weight, I stopped gaining muscle, and I flatlined.

It hasn't been until relatively recently that I've started to hit new personal records again. What's the difference? I've added a new regimen to my health tactics: strength training. But let me tell you, it hasn't been an easy thing to do. I dipped my toe in the water for months before I finally decided to commit to learning a new and better way of doing things. And this has made all the difference.

Consider a plane at takeoff. More energy and fuel are consumed during takeoff than at cruising altitude. There are a variety of reasons for this (power required to climb, thinning air at higher altitudes, and speed of travel while climbing versus cruising).

The same holds true for you and your day-to-day activities. Starting something new always requires more effort, therefore we simply don't. Most of us are comfortable with being complacent and simply cruising around our entire lives. But is that your ultimate objective?

If you're reading this book, you're probably after a bit more. That is going to require you to get over the fact that you're lazy, you tire quickly, and you want something for nothing. How do we do that? Simple: we choose. You can bury your head in the sand and pretend you're at the mercy of the environment, your associations, and your upbringing, or you can make a conscious choice to do more and be more. Don't fall prey to your natural desire to coast. Be deliberate, be intentional.

THE THIRD OPTION

One trap I see men fall into all the time is adhering to the idea that there are only one or two ways to do things. For example, one of the most commonly asked questions I get is, "Ryan, do you think I should take a job that would pay me more but require me to be on the road, or should I stay closer to my family but make less money?"

While I can appreciate the question, what the asker fails to realize is this is not an either/or conversation. It is possible to stay home and make more money. What's interesting to me is that when I bring this to the man who asked the question, I'm often met with a list of reasons why that won't work for him.

"Oh, but Ryan, you don't understand my situation."

"I would love to do that, but I need the money."

"That sounds great but there are no good-paying jobs near me."

"Wouldn't it be nice to have an online presence like you?"

"Great, but I don't have a college education."

The list is endless.

If you've caught yourself making any of these statements, you're more attached to your excuses than you are committed to being deliberate and intentional about your life. Let me be very clear about something: you get to keep what you defend.

If, for example, you think a college education is required to make money, you'll always live in poverty if you don't have a college degree.

If you think people are out to get you, you'll always put yourself in situations and surround yourself with people who are out to get you.

If you believe it's not possible to make money and be close to your family, you'll never have both.

See, you revert to your default thinking. And there is nothing intentional about that. Consider for just a second that, when met with two choices, there may be a third option you have yet to recognize.

The problem is that you've been living in a box. Hell, you are the box. Every experience, engagement, conversation, situation, belief, thought, book you've read, class you've attended, and sermon you've listened to has erected walls around the world you see.

To tear down those walls, or at least expand them, you're going to have to be a bit more intentional about how much or how little information you consume and where it's coming from. It's been said that knowledge is power. Even more accurate, options are power. We spend a lot of time restricting ourselves to limited solutions to our problems. A Sovereign Man is always looking for an alternative or an often-unseen solution.

THE MINDSET—EVERYTHING IN LIFE IS A CHOICE

Choices are powerful. Too bad most men spend their entire lives limiting them. We limit our choices through our thoughts and beliefs, the scripts we've chosen to believe, the echo chambers we create, the excuses we tell ourselves and others, and the power we give others over us.

Sovereignty is about recognizing that you have so many options available to you if only you would be more intentional about exercising them. Most men seem to be content with throwing up their hands and crying, "Well, there's nothing I can do about it!"

Wrong. There's always something you can do about it. There's always a choice to be made. There's always new information to be learned. There's always a new perspective in which to look at things.

Are you bold enough to tear down your preconceived ways of looking at things? Are you brave enough to expose the default answers you've always subscribed to? Are you strong enough to put your neck on the line and make a new choice to do something different?

Only when you can answer yes to these questions and recognize that your life is a series of choices can you truly say you're living with sovereignty.

THE SKILL SET

Make Up Your Mind. The single greatest skill set you could learn when it comes to living with intention is to make decisions. One of my pet peeves is when I ask my wife where she would like to go to dinner, only to be met with, "I don't know, wherever you want to go." Or, when I ask what she would like to do on a given evening, she responds with, "Whatever you want to do."

If you want to live your life with more intentionality, learn to be decisive and articulate what's on your mind. If the guys at the office ask where you want to go for lunch, tell them what you want for lunch. If your wife asks what you'd like to do this weekend, tell her what you'd like to do this weekend. Do not play coy. Be decisive.

Delegation. In addition to making decisions, the skill of delegating tasks you should not be doing is of the utmost importance. I'll admit, this is a skill set I am still improving. I've realized that if I am to do all that I am meant to do in my family, my business, and my community, I'm going to have to remove some things from my plate.

Yes, things have to get done, but there's no manual that says I have to be the one to do them. Learn to delegate. Learn to let go of the need to do everything. Learn to release control of the things that don't require your control. Only then will you be able to be intentional about the things that truly matter.

CHAPTER 9

DISCERNMENT

"The chief task in life is simply this: to identify and separate matters so that I can say clearly to myself which are externals not under my control, and which have to do with the choices I actually control."
-Epictetus

Everything is within your control. Sounds good, right? It's catchy. It's empowering. And it makes a great bumper sticker. Too bad it just isn't true. The reality is that there is a lot within your control—but not everything. The sooner you realize this and accept it for what it is, the sooner you give yourself permission to let go of the things beyond your control and focus only on what is.

This notion might sound counterintuitive, considering we're talking about wrestling control over your life, aka sovereignty. Although discerning what is within your control and what isn't won't give you more power over all of life's variables, it will give you power over the ones that actually matter.

Consider all that is outside of your control: your health, the economy, the weather, your favorite football team's performance last night, what other people do, what other people think of you, and on and on.

Yes, you may be able to influence these things, but you *cannot* control them. Attempting to do so is delusional, it's a waste of time, and it's a recipe for insanity. I can say that only because I used to live my life in delusion. I believed that the more I fought, the more I struggled, and the more I beat my head against the wall, the more likely I would be to get my way. It was exhausting and unsustainable.

The practice of focusing on the factors outside your control consumes your time, energy, focus, and attention, leaving you helpless when an opportunity actually presents itself.

If you've ever been to a Las Vegas magic show or seen a magician perform on the street, you've experienced this firsthand. No one actually believes that what these performers are doing is "magic." They're tricks. We know it. The magician knows it. And yet, it's difficult for us to expose the master's tactics.

Why? Because the magician knows how to manipulate your attention. You're so busy looking for the answer—and he's so well-versed in human behavior—that he makes you look left when you should be looking right. In that split second, the trickster performs his trick right in front of you, and you're left in awe to wonder how you could be so easily deceived.

We laugh and shrug it off because it's all fun and games. But what if your life is like one big magic show? What if there are forces at work that keep you from focusing your attention on where it should be? What if you are looking left when you should be looking right?

THE PATTERNS THAT DON'T EXIST

Our minds (and I believe this is especially true about men) are problem-solving machines. We are constantly on alert. We are constantly looking for potential threats. We are constantly looking for challenges to face.

It's the reason why women get upset with their husbands who attempt to fix what isn't broken. We know our wives are simply looking to vent, yet we cannot help the masculine urge to fix. My wife, for example, will often talk with me about a challenge she's having with one of her friends. I, being the "fixing" type, will offer suggestions to remedy the problem. Except there is no problem. She's simply telling me about her day. I'm making it worse by offering a solution to a problem that doesn't exist.

In the process of this natural desire to right the wrongs, our minds are constantly scanning for patterns to help us solve these complex problems. As a financial advisor, I could share with you story after story of investors who solved the equations to investing successfully in the stock market by uncovering hidden patterns inside sophisticated algorithms.

These equations all worked great, until they didn't. What appeared to be a pattern was nothing more than an illusion they had the audacity to believe was true. Once one new or previously unseen variable was entered into the equation, these prognosticators' false assumptions came crashing down.

The problem is we want so badly to be right. We want so badly to prove our value as men to the world. We want so badly to be admired and appreciated as we solve mankind's most elusive problems. All we really end up doing is banging our heads against the wall as we attempt to force a round peg into a square hole.

So, what do we do? We look for clues. We look for codes. We look for patterns that don't actually exist. We do all of this in a feeble attempt to assert our masculine dominance over our friends, family, neighbors, coworkers, and even strangers.

MEMENTO MORI

The ancient Stoics subscribed to the Latin phrase *memento mori*, which is translated as, "remember that you have to die." Although this may be a morbid notion on the surface, the Stoics—and many other philosophers and religions—chose for it to be a reminder of a way to live.

There is no escaping it—we are all going to die. That's outside of our control. What's inside our control is the way we choose to live our lives—our beliefs, our thoughts, and our actions.

The fear of death or any other factor outside our control can be a healthy fear. It's in our nature as a species to strive to stay alive. This is why we avoid taking unnecessary risks, dark spaces, and big spiders. It's when we take this fear to extremes that it becomes a problem.

In 2014, I took a business trip to New York. On the way home and about an hour outside of Denver, our plane hit a pocket of turbulence that caused the plane to drop violently. I immediately gripped the armrest and watched as those who were not buckled into their seats hit their heads on the ceiling of the airplane.

As everyone screamed and scrambled to get themselves buckled in, all I could do was think about what I hadn't done in my life. The things that went unsaid, the things that went undid, and the potential that remained untapped.

After things had calmed down, I peeled my fingers away from the armrest and took a couple of deep breaths. The gentlemen next to me asked the flight attendant how bad that was compared to what she had experienced in the past. She informed us that in fourteen years of flying, that was her scariest experience in a plane. To this day, the experience of that flight has altered the way I think about traveling. It has dictated when, where, and how I travel. And although it hasn't paralyzed me, it has certainly changed my perspective.

I'm not immune to the fear of death, but I know that basing our decisions off unnecessary fear (the risk of dying in a plane crash is 1 in 29,400,000) strips away our ability to make rational decisions, therefore limiting our choices and reducing our sovereignty.

Fearing death might keep you alive, but is it really any way to live? Subscribing to the phrase *memento mori* reminds us that, yes, we are going to die, so we might as well fully live.

William Wallace says it best in the movie *Braveheart* (can you tell what my favorite movie is yet?): "Aye, fight and you may die. Run, and you'll live . . . at least a while. And dying in your beds, many years from now, would you be willin' to trade *all* the days, from this day to that, for one chance, just one chance, to come back here and tell our enemies that they may take our lives but they'll never take *our freedom*!"

THE PAST, THE PRESENT, AND THE FUTURE

If there's one thing that humans know how to do very well, it's fret about things that have already happened or things that have yet to happen.

I'm often asked, if I could change one thing about my past, what would it be? I hate this question. I don't deal well in hypotheticals, and even if there was something I could change about the past, what good would it do? The fact is, I'm happy with my life, and, as the Butterfly Effect illustrates, changing just one detail about the past could potentially change everything about the present.

There's only one point of value in looking to the past. It doesn't have anything to do with reminiscing about your high school glory days or beating yourself up for your mistakes. What has already happened is simply a metric for determining your actions today. In other words, the past can teach us how we should operate now. That's it. It's a tool for learning. Dwelling on the past, however, has no bearing on what my future holds, and it certainly doesn't expand my options in the present.

It's a trap. The past will entangle the hearts and minds of men. I can hear Uncle Rico right now: "If coach would have put me in fourth quarter, we would have been state champions. No doubt. No doubt in my mind." We laugh, but we all know a friend who still defines himself by who he was nearly two decades ago. It's time to let go of the past. Remember the past, yes, but let go of it all the same.

At the opposite end of the spectrum, but equally uncontrollable, is the future. It makes sense why we as motivated, ambitious men would look to a future vision. In many ways, our ability to dream about what the future holds for us drives us to take the very actions that will get us there in the first place.

When our future vision drives us to action today, it becomes a powerful tool. It's when we get caught in that future vision that we unwillingly give up the power to choose and the power to do.

It's the same reason why excessive levels of entertainment (video games, movies, TV, sports, etc.) are damaging to the hearts and minds of men. Taken to the extreme, living vicariously through someone else's life (whether it's a professional athlete's or some delusional fantasy of the future you) entraps your mind and enslaves your soul. If you become content with romanticizing your life rather than living it, you risk shortchanging your potential.

Don't get lost in who you once were or who you have the potential to become. Use the past and the future to drive you to action today.

THE MINDSET—FOCUS ONLY ON WHAT YOU CAN CONTROL ———

Understanding that you cannot control everything is the first step. Accepting it is the second. Once you've come to terms with the reality that you cannot control everything, you can wrap your head around the notion of letting go.

It's fascinating that we try to take control of everything when most of us know full well we can't. Why do we do it? Why do we attempt to control what cannot be controlled? The simple answer: inadequacy and insignificance. We fear that, if we cannot control all the factors that go into our lives, somehow we are less than who we are supposed to be as men.

Genesis 3:19 says, "In the sweat of thy face shalt thou eat bread; till thou return unto the ground; for out of it wast thou taken: for dust thou art, and unto dust shalt thou return."

If that's true, it means we aren't as powerful as we think we are. It also means that we are at the mercy of the gods, the universe, or chance (however you choose to look at it).

It's a scary notion to live at the mercy of someone or something else. But the simple fact remains that there are certain things you can't do a damn thing about. Better to embrace the uncertainty of insignificance and focus only on what you can control.

THE SKILL SET

Daily Planning. At the crux of discernment is your ability to plan out every single day. If you have no idea what you're trying to accomplish, and how you're going to accomplish it, how can you be expected to know what's within your control and what's not?

I start every single day with my daily Battle Plan. I complete my six nonnegotiables (exercise, meditation, reading, journaling, planning, and visualization), list out the tasks I need to accomplish for the day, plan out my daily objectives (the results I'm after), and jot down any notes I may have about that day.

This foundation allows me to identify the actions I have control over and the actions I don't have control over, and it gives me the ability to focus my attention, efforts, and resources on the items within my power to control.

Tactic-Focused. When it comes to discerning between what you can do and what you can't, a tactic-centered approach is always going to be more effective than a goal-centered approach.

Most people fail because they focus too heavily on their goals.

Let's say, for example, you want to lose twenty pounds. If that goal is the extent of your planning, there are too many variables outside of your control that could potentially keep you from what you want to accomplish.

If, however, you focus on the tactics that will make that objective a reality, you're more likely to succeed. If my objective was to lose twenty pounds, I would focus on the tactics of drinking 100 ounces of water per day, exercising for at least one hour a day, and eliminating processed sugars.

Those three objectives will yield the desired result without having to focus on the result itself—just the tactics that are 100 percent within my control.

CHAPTER 10

WISDOM

"I am the wisest man alive, for I know one thing and that is that I know nothing."
-Plato

One phrase that gets tossed around a lot these days is "my truth." I understand what anyone who uses this phrase might be trying to say, but the reality is that there is no "my truth." There is only "the truth."

You might have a theory. You might have a perspective. You might have an assumption. But unless you're operating in objective reality, your opinion is just that—an opinion. Some might claim this is semantics. I disagree. Words are powerful. If you're distorting the meaning of a word or phrase to fit your narrative, you're likely limiting your perspective and your own sovereignty.

A Sovereign Man must strive to recognize, understand, and act according to objective truth—as in, the truth that is not subject to interpretation.

Let's say you were given the task of completing a big project at work. At the conclusion of the project, you determined your truth to be that you did a "good job" (subjective and open for interpretation) and communicated your accomplishments to your employer. You assumed he would be as ecstatic about the project as you are.

Unfortunately, you quickly find out he is not happy with your efforts and would like you to start the project over, or, worse, he assigns it to someone else.

If you're stuck believing the truth is that you did a good job, you will be less likely to do anything about improving the project or yourself. On the other hand, if you accept that what you only believed to be truth was merely a subjective opinion, and begin to consider other measurements for the successful completion of the project (time frame, budgeting constraints, results of the project, your employer's expectations, etc.), you have now given yourself the foundation from which to build and the sovereignty that comes with it.

This foundation from which to build is not an easy one to accept. Accepting the truth and acting upon it may require you to question everything you've ever known and everything you've ever believed about the way the world works. It may require you to accept that you've been wrong about a few things.

The question then becomes, are you more concerned with being right than you are about producing results? The Sovereign Man is driven by results, not his own ego or his ignorance.

IGNORANCE IS BLISS, OR IS IT?

As I mentioned before, there was a time when I weighed fifty pounds more than I do today. I was fat, I was exhausted, and I was miserable.

I will never forget the look of devastation on my son's faces when I had to tell them that I could not go jump with them on the trampoline. It wasn't that I didn't want to spend time with them. It was that I couldn't. Physically, I *could not*.

That was the day it clicked for me. I decided right then and there that I was going to get my health under control so I could step up more fully for my children and become more of the man I was meant to be.

Out of all the challenges I have faced on my road to wellness, it wasn't the working out that was the hardest. It wasn't getting out of bed earlier. It wasn't the discipline of doing the work. The hardest thing I had to do was to jump on the scale for the first time in five years.

I knew that it had gotten bad, but I had no desire to quantify how bad it actually was. It was easier for me to remain woefully ignorant than it was to face the reality of the situation I had created for myself.

You might be thinking, "C'mon, Ryan, why would that be so hard for you to do?"

Think about your life for a second. Have you ever avoided pulling up your bank account statement or retirement account because you knew what you'd find? Have you ever avoided a tough conversation with a boss or supervisor because you knew what he would have to say? Have you ever dodged a meaningful conversation with your wife because you knew things were on the rocks?

If the answer to those questions is yes, you too have fallen prey to turning a blind eye.

To overcome this natural tendency to pull the wool over your own eyes, you're going to have to grow up and stop acting like a child. Yes, I said, "stop acting like a child." Because when you pretend a situation doesn't exist that clearly does, frankly, you're acting like my four-year-old daughter.

The other night we took her to a Halloween corn maze. Each year, one of their employees dresses up as the headless horseman. He rode his horse up behind her but rather than scream, she simply threw her hands over her eyes and pretended the threat was no longer there.

Of course, covering our eyes does nothing to eliminate the threat, but it doesn't keep us from doing it either.

BECAUSE I SAID SO

If you're like me, there is no doubt that the phrase "because I said so" has passed your lips. I love that my children ask me questions, but sometimes it just gets to be too much. When I hit that line, my default answer is always, "because I said so."

If it works, my children stop asking questions and simply do what they're told to do. Unfortunately, I'm programming my children to avoid asking too many questions and training them to follow orders, not necessarily think for themselves.

We do this without thinking because our parents did it to us. This brings up an interesting consideration. As much as our children have the natural tendency to question and, in a way, rebel against authority, we have the same urge and desire.

You might be thinking, "I don't have the urge to rebel. I'm a team player. I get along with others and play nice." What if the only reason you do "play nice" is because the process of programming you to follow orders without asking questions is already complete?

Your parents, your teachers, your coaches, and your employers— bless their hearts—have spent decades conditioning you, prepping you, and getting you to follow orders. Sure, they might have your best interests at heart, but what started with noble intentions has now become a pattern for the way you operate your life—like a robot.

Nowhere is this more evident than in the military. I joined the military when I was eighteen, my senior year of high school. When I finished school, I shipped out to basic training in Fort Sill, Oklahoma.

From the minute we reached the Military Entrance Processing Station (MEPS), our life was no longer our own. For nearly four months, I was programmed and conditioned to act without thinking.

The day we officially started basic training, one poor private was gutsy (or dumb) enough to ask why we had to line up in formation.

I don't remember much of the answer to that question other than a slew of vulgar adjectives, five fired-up drill sergeants, and one sorry soldier.

I hold no ill will against the military for this training—in many ways, this type of programming has saved the lives of countless American soldiers. But there is no question that it was a battle for control of my heart and mind. Formations, cadence, inspections, and more were all designed to program me to adhere to a set of predetermined rules without question.

This sort of conditioning can be summed up perfectly in a scene from the movie *Forrest Gump*.

In the scene, Forrest Gump is assembling his weapon in the barracks.

"Done, Drill Sergeant," he yells.

The drill sergeant marches over and barks, "Guuump, why did you put that weapon together so quickly?"

Confused, Gump answers, "Because you told me to, Drill Sergeant." That's the perfect answer in the given moment, and one that is at direct odds with your agency.

One might make the argument this type of training is critical when it comes to the military and potentially life-or-death situations. The last thing you'd want in a firefight is someone questioning orders. Fortunately, for most of us, life isn't a series of life-or-death scenarios. That being the case, blindly following the pack means you've relinquished your sovereignty.

CONFUSION LEADS TO COMPLIANCE

One of the greatest threats to the powers that be is a wise man who operates in the world of objective reality. The wise man questions authority. The ignorant man pledges his blind allegiance. Who do you think is more profitable?

Big business knows this. The media knows this. The government knows this. And, whether you believe it's malicious or not, each of these organizations has created a web of confusion and complexity.

Take the financial industry, for example. I spent nearly a decade teaching consumers how the financial markets worked. In a way, I sat in a really interesting position. I was an insider to the financial companies I was expected to represent. I identified their motives. I studied their marketing strategies. I learned their language.

On the other hand, I had clients to represent. My clients paid me to offer products and solutions that would meet their financial objectives. In a way, I was the liaison between my clients and the products they wanted.

I can tell you from experience, the financial industry wants consumers in the dark. The more confused consumers are, the more profitable they become and the more reliant they are to the companies tugging on the strings.

When it comes to the media, consider the proliferation of fake news. We see false reports on everything from politics to professional sports, current affairs, and automobile maintenance.

The sad truth is that the mainstream media has become less about investigative journalism and more about outrageous, outlandish claims and headlines designed to get you to pay attention. It doesn't need to be true; it just needs to be captivating. The mainstream media may not be after your heart and soul, but they're after your eyeballs and attention.

With regard to the government, let's isolate just one element, the IRS. According to www.TaxFoundation.org, federal tax laws and regulations were over 10,000,000 words long in 2015, nearly six times longer than they were in 1955.

Why? Why does the tax code need to be so long? The answer is that it doesn't. There are ways not only to simplify tax code, but to make it much more efficient. But again, the more you're in the dark about the way things really work—the more confused you are—the easier it is to manipulate you.

Another clear indicator of the web of confusion is one element of the way we vote in the United States. For over two hundred years, our political environment has been dominated by a two-party system. For the most part, we vote either Republican or Democrat. Between the bickering, the constant attacks and insults hurled at the opposing party, and the magnification of these differences by the mainstream media, it has become nearly impossible to decipher which of our politicians believe what.

The solution? Straight-ticket voting. After all, why ask voters to critically analyze their politicians when you can simply make an option available to vote ALL Republican or ALL Democrat with a simple click of a button?

Whether it's big business, mainstream media, or our own government, at the end of the day, all the smoke and mirrors, all the confusion, and all the complexity is designed to get you to toe the line, to do what you're told, and to do it without question.

COMMON SENSE AND CRITICAL THINKING ARE THINGS OF THE PAST

Technology is amazing. It truly is. We have more access to information in the palm of our hands than ever before. With this technology comes many advancements in the way we work, communicate, and live.

However, one of the unintended consequences of this technology is that we have become a collection of the most informed morons the world has ever known. It's becoming painfully obvious that there is a huge lack of common sense and critical thinking, which has permeated much of society.

Several months ago, as I was scrolling through my Facebook feed, I came across two posts in particular. One post illustrated how a previous version of the iPhone lacked a headphone jack. One needn't worry though, as the illustration showed how to simply drill a port into your phone. The other post showed how adding a cup of sugar to your gas tank will keep the ethanol in your gas from freezing.

The sad part? In the comments, there were people who actually did what these posts suggested. Obviously (or so you would think), their phones and car engines were ruined.

Take another example: GPS. I've seen stories of people who, at the request of the GPS, stopped their vehicles in front of oncoming trains or drove their cars into lakes and rivers and even off the sides of cliffs.

Again, technology is not inherently bad, but when it comes at the expense of your own well-being, it's probably time we question our reliance on it and consider tapping into the supercomputer we all already possess: our brain.

KNOWLEDGE IS NOT POWER

Although critical thinking is an excellent starting point to regain some of the sovereignty we give away when we allow others to dictate what is right for us, it's not enough.

Knowing is never enough. We must do.

We've all heard the phrase "knowledge is power." That would be nice if it were true. It isn't.

What good, for example, does it do me to know how to write a book if I'm unwilling to actually write a book? The information, the ideas, and the knowledge that may be bouncing around in my brain do not serve me or anyone else if I am unwilling or incapable of turning that knowledge into the practical application of that knowledge.

Therefore, knowledge is not power; knowledge applied is.

We can see the negative ramifications of believing that only knowledge is required when we look at college students who spend four years or more to walk out of college with a liberal arts, religious studies, or philosophy degree. The education is great—so says the very institutions that have a vested interest in ensuring we believe it is—but at what cost did it come?

Congratulations, you now have more knowledge, but what could you have done with the time, money, and energy required to obtain it? This is known as lost-opportunity cost.

You could have started a business. You could have interned with a company and gained valuable experience. You could have been well on your way to making a difference instead of merely learning how to make a difference.

Is this always true? No. There are many careers in which a college education is extremely helpful and many careers where it simply isn't. I can't answer the question of whether or not you should go to college, but critically questioning that choice is something all men should do.

This process of evaluating your decisions is the critical distinction between knowledge and wisdom. Whereas knowledge is simply having the information, wisdom is the ability to discern what information is true and, more importantly, how it is applicable in your life.

THE MINDSET—RECOGNIZE AND ACT ACCORDING TO OBJECTIVE TRUTH

Wrapping your head around the idea that what you've been conditioned and programmed to avoid—asking too many questions about the truth of the way this world works—can be a daunting task. Couple that with the fact that it is often perceived as easier to bury our heads in the sand.

It may actually be easier . . . in the short term. But long term, truth always wins.

And because we're in this game for the long haul, we should always strive to play the long game. That game can only be won when we make a conscious effort to recognize and act according to objective truth—not to what our parents or teachers taught us, not to what the Internet says, but objective truth.

It's becoming increasingly challenging where everyone has a platform and everyone has something to say, whether or not they should. In many ways, the meteoric rise of social media has opened the world to many truths, while, at the same time, it has created a web of complexity and confusion that is hard to untangle.

As difficult as it has become and as magnified as the problem has yet to become, it is critical you do all you can to find the truth and act accordingly.

THE SKILL SET

Qualify Your Sources. As we've seen in recent years, the rise of "fake news" is creating some serious problems. That is compounded by the fact that many operate in a "herd mentality" and refuse to look objectively at the information they consume.

A Sovereign Man is an informed man. And he is not armed with just any information. He is armed with *accurate* information. In an age when people will believe anything they hear and see, when you consume new information, your first priority should be to qualify the source.

Ask yourself if the source is credible. Ask yourself what the source of this information has to gain by giving you said information.

Take the media, for example. What is their motive? Many would say it's to give you information. I disagree. Their motive is to get your attention so they can sell it to their advertisers. With that said, is it in their best interest to bore you with what may have actually happened or to sensationalize their stories?

I saw a video created by *USAToday* (what many would consider a credible source) that illustrated the components of an AR-15. In addition to the default components, it showed optional upgrades one could equip the firearm with. One of the optional upgrades they illustrated in the video was a chainsaw bayonet. I shit you not, a chainsaw bayonet. Are you kidding me? Get real. Unfortunately, there will be people who buy into that because "the Internet said so."

Question Everything. A healthy dose of skepticism goes a long way. Sure, this can be taken to the extreme. We all know that crotchety old man who believes in all the conspiracy theories and thinks everyone is out to get him. But skepticism in moderation is a healthy practice. Whenever I consume new information, I ask myself, "Is this really true?" I also attempt to find an alternate perspective that challenges the ideas I'm learning.

Aristotle says, "It is the mark of an educated mind to be able to entertain a thought without accepting it." Don't automatically assume because it's in a book or on the Internet, or because your wife's, brother's, friend's, uncle saw something, it's right or accurate. It may very well be, but your first response should always be to question it, analyze it, gain differing perspectives on it, and only then act on it.

CHAPTER 11

OWNERSHIP

"If we could change ourselves, the tendencies in the world would also change. As a man changes his own nature, so does the attitude of the world change towards him. This is the divine mystery supreme. A wonderful thing it is and the source of our happiness. We need not wait to see what others do."
-Mahatma Gandhi

An unfortunate reality of the world in which we live is a lack of men who have taken complete ownership of their lives. Everywhere you look you see countless men who have not only shirked their responsibilities as men, but who have pawned off any burden that comes with the mantle of masculinity.

"I got passed over for a promotion due to office politics," these men will say.

"I got a divorce because my wife didn't appreciate all that I did," they'll complain.

"I can't lose weight and get in shape because there's no gym near me," they'll gripe.

While some of that may be true, most men seem to be content with overlooking any responsibility and role they played in the situations in which they find themselves. But if there's one thing that makes a man a man, it's ownership. It's ownership of your thoughts, your beliefs, your actions, and ultimately the consequences that follow.

The dichotomy of ownership, however, is a challenging one to accept. When things go right, men have no problem accepting the praise and notoriety that come from a job well done. When things go wrong, however, that burden of responsibility is easily shifted to the people and situations seemingly outside their control.

You know exactly what I'm talking about. We've all had bosses who basked in the days of glory, but when the shit hit the fan, we were the first to be thrown under the bus. When things go wrong, how easy is it to say it's someone else's fault? How easy is it to blame our wife for the marital problems? How easy is it for us to blame the vendor for not getting the product out on time? How easy is it to blame the economy for our lack of financial resources?

Accepting responsibility and ownership of any given situation means accepting all of it, not just the victories.

WHEN A BOY BECOMES A MAN

First Corinthians 13:11 states, "When I was a child, I spake as a child, I understood as a child, I thought as a child: but when I became a man, I put away childish things."

Shifting blame and responsibility is the ultimate sign of a child. When I get after my oldest for hitting his brother, his immediate default answer is always, "It's not my fault; he started it." It's as if somehow, his younger brother forced him to hit him back.

We think, as men, we're above that behavior, but I can assure you, we're not.

I once watched a previous employer get after one of his team leaders for not completing a task on time. Rather than owning up to the fact that he didn't do what he said he would, the team leader immediately passed the blame to his team members, a vendor, and the economy.

I almost laughed out loud as I watched a grown man give the equivalent of my nine-year-old son's excuse: "Well, it's not my fault; he started it."

One of the questions I ask every guest of my podcast is, "What does it mean to be a man?" I've never heard two guests give the same answer, but I can say that the overwhelming majority of answers fall into the category of responsibility and ownership.

Contrast this with my three sons, who are nine, six, and two. They're boys, not men. They're not even expected to be. Sure, they have some chores to do around the house. They have to practice the piano and go to football practice, but at the end of the day, the burden of responsibility of ensuring these things get completed falls on me as their father and the man of the house.

But make no mistake, being a man has less to do with age than one might think. One hundred years ago, boys were expected to step up as men far earlier than they are now. If a father passed away, many times, young boys would drop out of their schooling to go to work full-time to help make ends meet at home. In other words, they assumed responsibility. The flip side of that coin is the thirty-year-old man who still plays video games while living in his mommy and daddy's basement.

Being a man has less to do with age and more to do with the ownership of your own lives and the lives of those under your care. But in order to step into that role of Sovereign Man, you're going to have to understand that every position you find yourself in is your fault.

IT'S ALL YOUR FAULT

Yes, I said it: "It's all your fault."

Your financial situation is your fault.

Your level of health is your fault.

Your relationship status is your fault.

Everything about your life is your fault.

There are situations outside your control (refer to Chapter 9, "Discernment"), but you are always in control of how you respond to these situations.

Let's break down the examples from above.

FINANCES

"Ryan, my broker screwed me." You didn't do your research.

"I lost money in my 401(k) because of the economy." Then explain to me how other people made money during the same time. Maybe you just didn't diversify well enough.

"I got injured and I can't work anymore. It's not my fault but now we're in debt." Why didn't you set money aside for a rainy day?

HEALTH

"There's no gym near me." Who said you need a gym to be healthy?

"Eating healthy requires more money than eating poorly." No, it doesn't. It just requires a little bit of planning. Besides, how much money do you spend on Netflix, cable, and quick trips to the convenient store?

"I wish I could lose weight, but I'm just big boned. I can thank my parents for that." First, your bones are the same size as everyone else's. Second, if genetics is something you have to deal with, you might just have to work a little harder at it than others.

RELATIONSHIPS

"Ryan, you don't understand, my wife is a bitch." Maybe, but you married her.

"Yeah, but she's changed since we got married." So have you.

"My wife doesn't believe in the new business I'm starting." You can't even take out the trash when you say you will. Why should she trust you with the family's livelihood?

I'm not denying that some of what you deal with is caused by someone or something else. What I am saying is, what you're telling yourself just isn't the complete truth. Parts of your scripts may be true, but you're leaving out the critical elements that give you the power to actually do something about it.

When you're selective with your stories, you give away the power and sovereignty you have to make a difference in your life and the lives of those you care about. You put yourself at the mercy of the winds, chance, or fate.

YOU HAVE THE POWER

You are powerful. More powerful than you give yourself credit for. More powerful than even you would like to admit.

It's been said that with great power comes great responsibility, which is why most people run away from that power. We give it away. We ignore it. We hide from it.

I hear people say that accepting too much of the burden and responsibility is a mistake, especially when it's truly not your fault or problem. I think it's a mistake not to accept the burden of responsibility. Most people think responsibility is limiting. I think it's empowering.

If I pawn off the success of my business, my finances, my health, and my relationships on other people, I hinder my ability to expand and grow. Essentially, I've put myself at the mercy of other people, their baggage, and their agendas.

But when I accept that I have the ultimate responsibility to myself and to others for my business, my finances, my health, and my relationships, I have now positioned myself for the growth and expansion that can only come through critical thinking and intentional action.

No longer am I at the mercy of whatever life may have to offer. I have an active part in creating the life I desire. And to wrestle control back of the ultimate power you possess, you're going to have to let go of the excuses you love to conjure up.

NO EXCUSES, DRILL SERGEANT

Excuses are crafty. They feel so real. They feel legitimate. But they're not. They're lies, plain and simple. And they pose a very real and dangerous threat to your heart and mind.

Our excuses are so easily disguised, and they're so difficult to detect. Therefore, it becomes necessary to take drastic measures. You must declare a "zero tolerance" policy on your excuses. Personally, I've adopted a mantra that I learned nearly twenty years ago.

When I joined the military in 1999, I was fortunate enough to begin training with my unit prior to shipping off to Basic Training. Among other things, I learned the ranks, how to wear my uniform, and some of the basics of the job I would be performing. But one thing that was etched into my brain as I prepared for my formal training was the phrase "No excuses, Drill Sergeant."

If ever I got into trouble, I was to utter the words, "No excuses, Drill Sergeant."

If ever I did something dumb, I was to recite the words, "No excuses, Drill Sergeant."

If ever I found myself at the receiving end of an angry trainer, I was to repeat the words, "No excuses, Drill Sergeant."

Looking back on my experience, I can remember having to say those words only once. I can't remember what I did or why I had a drill sergeant crawling up my ass, but I do remember the look of shock and silence on my drill sergeant's face when I looked him in the eyes and said, "No excuses, Drill Sergeant." He stopped, looked me up and down, and simply said, "Good. Carry on, Private." What could have turned into an hour-long "smoke session" by this seasoned professional turned out to be just a slap on the wrist. I had caught him off guard with something, apparently, he wasn't used to hearing.

That's the day I learned that a man doesn't make excuses. He doesn't create stories. He doesn't shift blame. He simply accepts his ass-kicking, learns from his mistakes, and drives on.

THE MINDSET—ACCEPT RESPONSIBILITY FOR YOUR THOUGHTS, YOUR ACTIONS, AND THEIR CONSEQUENCES

Taking complete ownership of your life is not an easy thing to do, especially if you've been passing the buck your entire life. But it's an absolute requirement if you have any hope of accomplishing big things and recapturing your heart and mind.

Come to terms with the fact that you're going to be wrong, that you don't have it all figured out, and that you don't need to.

When you win, own it. You deserve it. When you lose, own it. You deserve it.

Realize also that people aren't going to think less of you when you accept full responsibility for your thoughts, ideas, and actions. If anything, people are going to respect you more when you're willing and able to say, "I'm sorry. That was my fault and I will correct it."

That statement does not limit you. It empowers you to correct the thoughts, actions, and patterns you've exercised in your life. It's the foundation for growth. It's not an opportunity to beat yourself up; it's an opportunity to learn.

When you do finally accept that everything is within your control and you're willing to shoulder the burden of owning your life, you give yourself permission to thrive and the right to call yourself a man.

THE SKILL SET

After-Action Review. The After-Action Review is a tool I learned in the military. It's an exercise I use after every engagement, encounter, conversation, project, and assignment. Simply put, it's a series of five questions designed to critically analyze and evaluate any given scenario. It's also designed to give you the feedback needed to empower you to own the shortcomings of the project and tighten up anything that needs to be improved.

The five questions are:

- What did I accomplish that I set out to accomplish?
- What did I not accomplish that I wanted to?
- What did I do well in this exercise/project/etc.?
- What did I not do well in this exercise/project/etc.?
- What will I do better next time?

I encourage you to write these questions down and refer to them often. Soon, and through repetition, you will internalize these questions and use them to focus on the actions that propel you forward.

Empowering Questions. Outside of the After-Action Review, focus on improving the questions you're asking yourself on daily basis.

Instead of asking, "Whose fault is this?" ask yourself, "What can I do to ensure this doesn't happen again?"

Instead of asking, "Why didn't _____ do _____ ?" ask yourself, "What can I do to ensure _____ gets done next time?"

Instead of asking, "Why am I surrounded by incompetent people?" ask yourself, "What can I do to surround myself with competent people?"

The first set of questions does nothing to improve the situation. The second set of questions focuses on what you can do to improve the situation.

It's been said that the quality of your life will be determined by the quality of the questions you ask. Make your questions count.

CHAPTER 12

STRENGTH

"Strong men greet war, tempest, hard times. They wish, as Pindar said, to tread the floors of hell, with necessities as hard as iron."
-Ralph Waldo Emerson

Believe it or not, there was a time when men were strong—mentally, emotionally, physically. Yes, I say that a little tongue-in-cheek, but one needn't look very far to see that the strength we once possessed as men seems to be dying out. While it may be a condition of the times in which we live, our obligation to protect, provide, and preside has not subsided in the least.

The idea of masculine strength has been replaced with the notion of "vulnerability" and a man who's "in touch with his feelings." While I can agree there is a place and a time for a man to understand his emotions and what he is dealing with (refer to Chapter 16, "Self-Awareness"), it should never come at the expense of accomplishing the task at hand.

I'm often told that a man isn't defined by his muscles. I agree. But he certainly isn't defined by his ability to be in touch with his sensitive side. A man is defined by what he does or, more specifically, by the outcome of what he does. Intentions are great; results are what matter.

That said, when a man chooses to overlook his need to be strong on every front, results falter. Throughout your life, you will be called upon to shoulder some heavy burdens: bankruptcy, divorce, layoffs, disease, disability, etc. When a man is weak, his ability to shoulder those burdens becomes unbearable and everyone loses.

Unfortunately, strength seems to have become a luxury reserved for those who have the time and inclination to simply look the part. The fitness industry, for example, has been infiltrated by marketing tactics that sound really good but accomplish very little when it comes to actually being stronger. "10 Belly-Blasting Exercises in 10 Minutes" is a headline I recently read, as if six-pack abs are the great metric of man's overall level of health.

Even worse is the annoyingly overused word "alpha." What exactly is an "alpha" anyway? Here we have another example of a cleverly worded marketing campaign designed to make a man feel strong rather than develop the strength he only wishes he had. It's like the old adage goes, "If you have to tell people you are, you aren't."

THE WORLD HAS GONE SOFT

Unfortunately, our society has attempted (rather poorly, I might add) to strip away any need to develop the type of mental, emotional, and physical strength our great ancestors possessed. One example where we can clearly see this is youth sports.

When I became a father for the first time, I made a commitment to coach as many of my children's sports teams as possible. Now, with two boys who each play three sports per year, it's become a difficult promise to uphold. Regardless, I find it fascinating that we don't keep score—even for my nine-year-old. Why? Why are we so afraid to teach our children they will fail? Why are we so afraid of measuring their success, or lack thereof, in real time through keeping score? Why are we so afraid that little Timmy and Tommy won't be able to bear a brutal beatdown by another, better team?

Interestingly enough, since the time my boys were three years old, they've been asking after the game what the score is. They want to know. They want to learn. They want to prove themselves strong enough.

This desire for males to prove themselves worthy doesn't end when we're children. But every time society says we don't need to keep score, let's give participation trophies to every child, and let's do everything we can to ensure that our children don't have to push themselves, we rob them of the opportunity to develop the strength they need to endure all the real world has to offer as they become men.

The natural result is men who are incapable of coping and dealing with the difficulties I mentioned above: bankruptcy, divorce, layoffs, disease, disability, etc. Take a look at suicide rates, for example. Some studies suggest that suicide rates among men are as much as three times higher than those of women. Most would have you believe it's because we've been telling men to "man up" for too long, but I'd suggest it's because we haven't been equipping ourselves with the mental fortitude, emotional resiliency, and physical strength needed not only to survive but to thrive.

INOCULATION

In 2005, I found myself preparing to leave on a deployment to Iraq. Among the list of preparations was a series of shots we were given to keep us safe from any disease we might experience through either being in a new environment or biological warfare.

Among these shots was the smallpox vaccine. The smallpox vaccine (and many others) is considered a "live virus" vaccine. I remember receiving my vaccine. A medic pulled a sizable needle from his kit and stabbed my left shoulder. Once inserted into my arm, the needle was rotated several times in a circular pattern. This was repeated three times.

The reason for this process is that a virus (similar to smallpox but less harmful) was being introduced to my body. The introduction of a live virus is designed to help the body develop an immunity to smallpox. For the first couple of days, I experienced headaches, nausea, and swollen lymph nodes (especially in my armpits). Eventually these symptoms subsided as my body developed the ability to resist and fight the virus. Now, I am immune to smallpox.

As painful and unenjoyable as that process was for me, it's incredible that the body has the ability to develop the resources required to fight disease. But that's not all the body can do. The body can inoculate itself against a variety of conditions we're all likely to experience: heartbreak, heartache, failure, rejection, setback, injury, depression, etc. One simply needs to introduce the "virus" and watch the body, mind, and heart do what it does best.

See, most of us spend our entire lives running from anything that could potentially pose a threat. It's understandable. At the core of the human condition is a burning desire to stay alive. But here's the deal: most of what scares you isn't going to kill you. It's simply going to make you uncomfortable for a while until that stressor—in whatever form—becomes the new standard by which you judge other difficulties.

ADVERSITY IS YOUR ALLY

For this reason, and in order to develop the mental fortitude, emotional resiliency, and physical strength required to recapture and maintain your sovereignty, I would have you consider running toward adversity as opposed to away from it.

Don't get me wrong, I'm not suggesting that you run toward danger, but rather you run toward discomfort. Anything good that has ever come into my life has been the direct result of some level of discomfort. It's been said that nothing worth having comes easy.

Just as I experienced the painful symptoms of my inoculation against smallpox, a man must experience the pain and uneasiness that come from embracing what scares him most. It's part of the process.

To illustrate the point, consider the blacksmithing forging process. A piece of raw metal is introduced to fire. The fire burns hot enough that the metal becomes soft and pliable, at which point it is pulled from the fire. Once pulled from the fire, the raw metal is hammered, twisted, chiseled, and formed into the resemblance of the desired shape. This process is repeated over and over again until the blacksmith has his roughly finished piece.

Next, a series of wheels, stones, files, and wire brushes, along with yet another heat treatment, is used to finalize the piece and ensure the master has achieved the desired hardness of the newly forged metal.

As the blacksmith forges raw metal in the refining fire, you must also jump into the refining fire of life by deliberately placing yourself in challenging situations. This is the only way to become stronger mentally, emotionally, and physically.

MENTAL FORTITUDE

At the crux of a man's strength is his ability to fortify his mind. Everything we have and everything we are in life is formed first in the mind. In order to see what you're fully capable of, you're going to have to put your assumptions about how tough you are to the test.

To draw upon my experience in participating in the Spartan Agoge once again, the physical pain I experienced as my soles were separating from my feet was insignificant compared to the internal battle that was being waged in my mind.

I remember one instance in particular. We were roughly twenty-six hours into the sixty-hour ordeal and had just been awakened by Spartan founder Joe De Sena after a measly hour and a half of rest. Upon jolting us from our desperately desired sleep, Joe had us form a circle. Once the circle was complete, Joe demanded that we give him a hundred burpees if we wanted to stay in the event.

"A *hundred* burpees?" I thought. "There's no way I can do this!"

"Ready, begin!" Joe barked.

We got to twenty burpees before Joe interrupted, "No! You're doing them wrong. Start over!"

Again we started and again, after twenty burpees, Joe yelled, "No! You're not doing them together as a team. Start over!"

"*Shit!*" I thought. "It's okay, you got this," I desperately tried to convince myself over the sound of the participant next to me puking his guts out.

Eventually, we managed to get our hundred burpees in. It wasn't pretty, but it was done. What had seemed impossible in my mind just a few minutes earlier was not impossible after all but simply a mental barrier my mind had fabricated to keep me comfortable.

After we completed our burpees, Joe had a proposition for us. From the center of the circle, he said, "If you'd like to quit now, no one will think less of you. Everyone here will wish you on your way. Hopefully, you got what you came for and have grown from this experience. However . . . ," he continued, "if you decide to stay and commit to seeing this through, from this point on, if just one person quits, no one here finishes the event."

That was a difficult decision to make. On one hand, I was in pain. I felt as if I was in over my head and this was the perfect opportunity for me to bail. On the other hand, I had committed to seeing this thing through. I had told our Facebook group of roughly thirty thousand men that I would hit sixty hours. More compelling than that was the text I received from my wife just before starting the event. She had sent me a picture of my children, who had made signs that read, "Go Dad! We know you can do it. See you in 60 hours."

No way in hell was I quitting. They were going to have to drag me off that field before I threw in the towel. After committing to myself and the team that I would finish, things became easier. It was hard, no doubt, but mentally I had removed any backup plan, any plan B, any escape route. I had burned the ships, so to speak.

That sixty hours in the mountains of Vermont changed me. It challenged my previously held beliefs and the scripts I had been playing over and over in my mind.

"Ryan, you can't do this."

"You're not good enough."

"You're not strong enough."

Bullshit. I had proved to myself that I was, in fact, capable of more than I had ever given myself credit for. There was no denying it. It was done.

And therein lies the power of deliberately placing yourself in mentally challenging positions, of testing yourself. You've been telling yourself stories about how strong you are mentally. But the fact is you don't really know. You can't know until you're willing to step up to the plate and see how far you really can go.

Developing mental fortitude cannot be done with your nose in a book. It cannot be dreamed about or imagined. It cannot be wished for, hoped for, or prayed for. It cannot be vicariously lived through others. The only way to fortify the mind is to place it under stress, heat, and duress—like the refiner's fire.

EMOTIONAL RESILIENCY

Equally important to mental fortitude is emotional resiliency. Look, life is tough. You're going to lose. You're going to fail. People are going treat you unfairly. At times, you're going to be dealt an unfair hand. These situations are hard enough as it is, but when compounded with a lack of emotional intelligence, understanding, and restraint, you're all but guaranteed to fail.

It's critical you understand that the world is not against you. It's not necessarily for you, either. It just . . . is. Wrapping your head around the notion that the world (or the universe or any other way you choose to define it) is neutral and that relatively few people care about you either way gives you the foundational understanding needed to treat emotions for what they are: indicators.

That's right, emotions are simply a metric for what is happening in your life. Just as the gauges on the dashboard of your vehicle indicate how fast you're going, how far you've gone, and how warm your engine is, emotions indicate what's working well, what's not working, and where some things are off in your life.

When you give emotions more credit than they deserve, you unwittingly relinquish the control you have to choose your own path. You would never blame your odometer for how fast or slow you're driving. You'd place the burden of responsibility on yourself for how hard you're pressing on the gas pedal. You would never blame your fuel level indicator for running out of gas. You would blame yourself for overlooking the importance of filling up the gas tank.

When you allow your emotions to get the better of you because someone flipped you off as you were driving or you started feeling sorry for yourself because your boss doesn't like you, you're blaming the symptom (anger, greed, resentment, bitterness, etc.) for the root cause of the problem. In this case, it could simply be that you drive like an asshole and you aren't as productive at work as you think you are.

That's a difficult pill to swallow, but isn't that better information? Choosing to be offended because someone suggested you're a bad driver via a certain nonverbal communication is insignificant to the actual understanding you can't drive worth a shit. The former keeps you where you are. The later allows you to grow.

This is why emotional resiliency is an absolute must on the journey to your own sovereignty. Allowing others or outside situations to dictate how you're feeling is a sure path to bondage. The desire and ability to use those feelings as simple metrics to produce a desired outcome is much more powerful.

PHYSICAL STRENGTH

To complete the trifecta of masculine strength, we turn to physical strength. Bottom line, strong men can do more. Is it possible to be a good man and not be strong? Yes. Is it possible to fully be the man you're meant to be if you're not strong? No.

In his book *The Way of Men*, Jack Donovan makes the distinction between being a good man and being good at being a man. Being "good at being a man" requires physical strength. Strong men have the capacity to work harder, longer, and more effectively. At the end of the day, strong men produce.

In 2015, I was the heaviest I've ever been. I was topping the scales at 235 pounds and, for a man who stands only five foot ten, it was not a pretty sight. As many excuses as I came up with, I could not deny the fact that my physical health was affecting my ability to produce results on every front of my life: business, wealth, relationships, etc.

I remember at that point in my life receiving a flyer for CrossFit. The owners were opening a new gym near me. I decided enough was enough; it was time for me to do something about my failing physical health.

Up until that point, I had always been physical. I lettered in three sports in high school. I never had any problems performing in the Army Physical Fitness Test (APFT). I knew getting back in shape wouldn't be a problem, but what I didn't realize was the unintended positive consequences of getting my ass back in gear.

This isn't a book about physical fitness. I don't know what exercise regimen or diet program is going to work best for you. I personally participate in CrossFit, Starting Strength, and Spartan Races, and, as far as nutrition goes, I eat clean (limited processed sugars, lots of vegetables, lean meats, and plenty of water). What works for you may be the same or it may be entirely different. Either way, I'd encourage you to check out the vast collection of health-related material online, in books, or through gym memberships and fitness coaching.

What I can tell you is that since 2015, when I set out on this fitness journey, my life has drastically improved. My financial planning began to grow; the Order of Man has exploded; my wealth has increased substantially; and my relationships with my wife, children, and friends have never been better.

Some might claim that I've figured something else out—that the results I've experienced in my life are correlated with new information or access to an expanding network. That may be true to a degree, but none of that would have happened had I not developed the skill set to improve my health, which was, interestingly enough, the same skill set required to thrive in every other area of my life: dedication, discipline, commitment, hard work, sacrifice, and resiliency.

Often, men who feel they have lost their way ask me, "Where should I start this journey to improve?" My answer is, "The gym. It all starts in the gym."

THE MINDSET—I AM MENTALLY TOUGH, EMOTIONALLY RESILIENT, AND PHYSICALLY STRONG

The unfortunate reality is that we are designed to look for the path of least resistance. In many ways, our natural inclination to choose the easy route is the exact factor that has kept us alive and thriving as a species for thousands of years.

But as new advancements in health, comfort, and technology continue to develop, the likelihood of running across a scenario that will kill us is drastically reduced. While the easy route may be comfortable, the hard route is what builds the mental fortitude, emotional resilience, and physical strength required to step fully into our role as men. The easy route makes us weak. The hard route makes us strong.

To become a man of strength, you must wrap your head around and adopt the mantra "I embrace the challenge." I was in my home gym this morning, doing a particularly heavy set of squats. The programming called for four sets of five squats. I had just completed my fourth rep in the third set when my mind said, "Ryan, that's good enough. You can call it quits here." I almost fell prey to the easy route as I caught myself racking the weight. When I realized what I was doing, I repeated the mantra in my head, "I embrace the challenge." I lifted the bar back off the rack and completed the set. As trivial as that experience may sound, I'm a better man for it.

Deciding whether to finish the set is one of hundreds, if not thousands, of choices we will be faced with throughout the day. Your natural tendency will always be to choose the path of least resistance. You must fight the urge to take the easy route and, instead, embrace the challenge.

THE SKILL SET

Make the Hard Path the Easy Path. Understanding that we have a natural tendency to choose the easy path can be used to our advantage. Many times, we understand that choosing to do something hard is the better route, but we place so many barriers between where we are and where we want to be that the task becomes almost impossible to complete.

When I set out on my fitness journey three years ago, one of the biggest challenges for me was getting out of bed and into the gym. I didn't know what workout I was going to do. I didn't want to get my gym clothes out. I didn't want to get my water and/or pre-workout ready. So I stayed in bed.

To combat this, I simply programmed my workouts the night before and had my gym bag ready and my drink waiting for me in the fridge. When I woke up in the morning, I had no excuses.

Take some time to understand what barriers are keeping you from achieving what you want and find a way to tear them down ahead of time.

Reset the Default. Our default answer is always "whatever is easier." We all know this and have been abiding by it for so long that we rarely give ourselves the chance to critically analyze if that's the right answer at all. What if, instead, we reprogrammed our thought process to respond with "whatever is the hardest" as the default answer?

I'm not suggesting it always will be, but choosing the hard thing first will force you to stop and actually think about what you should be doing in the first place. It will also give you the opportunity to consider the mantra "I embrace a challenge."

CHAPTER 13

HUMILITY

"It is impossible for a man to learn what he thinks he already knows."
-Epictetus

The longer I'm alive, the more I realize how little I actually know. Sure, I like to put on a front. All of us feel good when we know what we're talking about. But make no mistake, there is a huge difference between knowing what we're talking about and thinking or, even worse, pretending we know what we're talking about.

Knowing what we're talking about requires effort. Through this effort to gain new understanding, and with a desire and ability to act on that understanding, we earn the right to that knowledge. However, pretending we know what we're talking about requires only deceit.

Doesn't it feel wonderful to deceive? When we trick people into thinking we know more than we do, we receive the accolades and praise of the unsuspecting victims of our deceit. Just as damaging is the fact that we deceive ourselves. When a man lies to himself about how much he actually knows, he robs himself of the opportunity to learn new information that would propel his life forward rather than simply make him feel good about himself in the moment.

Why then do we, as men, work so hard to maintain the appearance of knowledge? One word: ego. To put it frankly, we refuse to look foolish. Therefore, we'd prefer to run the risk associated with making something up rather than appearing dumb.

Somewhere along our journey from boys to men, we transform from "inquisitive" to "know-it-all." We begin to worry about what others think of us and how we portray ourselves to the people we care about. Couple that with the fact that society would have you believe you should know it all and that, somehow, if you don't already know how to do X, Y, and Z, you're not a "real man."

As evidence, you see that most of society does not mock toddlers when they fall or young boys when they mispronounce a word. They're not expected to know it all, so they get a pass. But there comes a time in our lives when the passes expire. When that day comes, we do the only thing we know how to do when we don't know the answer: we make something up.

We lie because we remember the first time someone mocked or ridiculed us for not knowing. Rather than experience the feeling of embarrassment or rejection again, we utilize one of our most basic and frequently used defense mechanisms—our imagination.

That's all an ego is, anyway—it's delusion, it's a fantasy land. We begin to create a false reality in our own minds about how good we are and how much we actually know. If we tell ourselves something long enough, we start to believe it. This tactic preserves our ego, but it destroys our sovereignty. We become slaves to ourselves and the egomaniacs we create.

I know how this works firsthand. As I was building my financial planning practice, I was trained to give all the answers (whether or not I actually knew them). If I didn't know the answer, I was expected to make something up. Heaven forbid I ever tell a client, "I don't know."

That's what I did, day in and day out. I put on the nice suit, I kept my face shaved, I wore my hair just right, and I said all the right things. And I deceived myself. I placed so much pressure on myself to be the kind of man that everyone told me I should be, but inside I knew this wasn't real and I wasn't happy with who I had become.

HUBRIS

Man's desire to keep his ego safe is nothing new. Naturally, we've been engaging in this behavior since the dawn of man. The ancient Greeks used the word "hubris" to define someone who exhibited extreme foolishness or dangerous overconfidence. In Greek mythology, Nemesis was the goddess who delivered retribution for those who displayed hubris. Proverbs 16:18 says, "Pride goeth before destruction, and a haughty spirit before a fall." It seems everywhere we turn we are warned of the destructive consequences of an inflated ego.

In 2006, I had just returned from Iraq and begun my career in the financial industry. I was nervous but excited to enter a new chapter in my life, and, although I had never done anything in this line of work before, I was confident in my ability to succeed.

I had always enjoyed relative success in anything that I engaged in. I started varsity football as a sophomore, lettered in three sports, consistently made honor roll, graduated at the top of my class in Advanced Individual Training in the Army, earned a promotion to store manager from part-time employee, and ran a successful retail clothing store my company had asked me to open. Surely, this venture wouldn't be any different.

It wasn't long before the reality of the situation hit me. My first year in the business, I made roughly $30,000; my second-year earnings weren't much more; and by the third year, I was ready to throw in the towel.

Every night, I would come home from work upset, exhausted, and defeated. I would wander out to our backyard and pace around the perimeter while I wondered how I was going to make the mortgage payment. It was a humbling time in my life.

I looked around at the other agents in my office who were experiencing success and wondered how they were doing it. I told myself I was just as good as, if not better than, them.

"How do they get so lucky with their clients?" I would silently complain. It had to be luck. I was good. There was no way my lack of results could possibly have anything to do with me.

Fortunately for me, I had no fallback plan. I had to make this work. There was nothing else to do. So, as I contemplated quitting and moving on, I decided to try one more thing and do something I wasn't used to doing: I asked for help.

ASKING FOR HELP

During my third year in my financial planning practice, I had identified several advisors in my office who were perpetual performers. It did not seem to matter what was going on in the market, what time of year it was, or what the political environment happened to be. Regardless of outside circumstances, these few men seemed to have figured out something I had not.

With all the courage I could muster (and without a plan B), I approached these advisors and asked if I could take them to lunch and ask a few questions. It was humiliating. For the first time in my life, I had to tell someone else that I had no idea what the hell I was doing and that I needed guidance.

To my surprise, each of these men accepted my offer and spent time with me over lunch, teaching me some of their tactics and strategies. Eventually, I asked them to go on client appointments with me. At the time, I didn't have the money to pay them to coach me, so I suggested that we split any revenue from the clients we worked together with. This was a hard pill to swallow as I was barely making ends meet. But I realized 100 percent of zero is still zero.

It wasn't long before I was picking up new clients and making more money than I ever had in the business, even after the split. Today, and with the help of those early coaches, I've turned my financial planning practice into a six-figure business.

Sometimes all it takes is the courage to ask for help.

I understand why we don't. We're afraid. We're afraid because we've been conditioned to believe that we can't ask for help without being thought less of. Our parents, teachers, coaches, employers, clients, friends, and colleagues, with all their good intentions, have crippled us into believing that if we ask for help, we're not good enough or worthy of the relationship we have with them.

Asking for help is a risk. "What if people laugh at me?" "What if people mock me?" "What if people think less of me?" We ask ourselves these questions and worse.

Not asking for help is a sure bet. It may not produce the desired result, but at least we don't have to expose our own vulnerabilities, weaknesses, and inadequacies.

But I'd have you consider that the greater threat lies not in asking for help, but in failing to live up to the potential that is locked inside you. Most men live their entire lives less than they're capable of simply because they'd rather maintain their pride than admit they aren't as smart as they think they are.

What an unfortunate reality. How many promotions have been lost? How much money has been left on the table? How much knowledge has been overlooked? How many opportunities have passed you by? All to maintain the appearance of power rather than the actual power that comes from recognizing, admitting, and doing something about the fact that you don't know it all.

HUMILITY IS STRENGTH

Most men believe that simply appearing powerful garners the attention, respect, and admiration of others, along with all the accompanying benefits. While this may be true temporarily, the long-term consequence of an inflated ego is a level of suspicion and doubt among those a man works so hard to impress.

I've seen plenty of men who appeared to be strong only to reveal, down the road, that they were hiding their inadequacies and over-compensating for their lack of true understanding.

We hear phrases like "fake it 'til you make it" and begin to believe that pretending to know the answers will yield the desired results. This couldn't be further from the truth. In fact, if anything, overconfidence moves us further away from the results we're after.

When we "fake it," we give ourselves permission to neglect gaining the knowledge, information, skills, tools, and experience required to produce the long-term benefits of having a firm grasp of the knowledge we only pretend to have.

What if, instead of believing that arrogance is strength, we wrapped our head around the fact that it's humility that makes us strong? Consider the characteristics tied to humility—inquisitive, realistic, likable, approachable, optimistic, educated, open-minded—versus the characteristics of arrogance—close-minded, ignorant, delusional, guarded, deceitful, pessimistic.

See, when guys put on a front or show to maintain their pride, what they really end up doing is exposing themselves to all sorts of blind spots that could come back to destroy them. You hear of guys all the time who get blindsided with a separation or divorce or lay-off, or they're hit with news that someone else got the promotion.

I used to think these guys were complete morons if they couldn't see some of this stuff happening. While I know we all get hit with surprises, I can't help but think that if we get hit with surprise after surprise after surprise, we've got to be delusional about what's really going on around us.

That's what this false sense of pride, ego, and arrogance create—delusion, a false reality about how good we actually are and all the wonderful things we're doing in the world.

CONFIDENCE VERSUS ARROGANCE ─────────────────────

Pride is a good thing. It's important that we take pride in what we do and remain confident in our abilities, but there's a huge difference between confidence and arrogance.

So what *is* the difference between confidence and arrogance? The answer is simple: confidence is earned; arrogance is not.

As easy as it is to take pride to an unhealthy level, it is just as easy to take humility to an unhealthy level. A humble man is not someone who can be pushed around, stepped on, and manipulated to do the will of others. A humble man is one who knows his shortcomings and is consciously working on improving them. It is absolutely possible to be both humble and confident. After all, for all your shortcomings, you also possess many strengths. A humble man is fully capable of recognizing both.

I, for example, thrive behind a microphone and a camera. That's not arrogance. It's confidence. The right to acknowledge the skill of communicating via video and audio is not something I take lightly or take for granted. In fact, for the longest time, I struggled with both. Only through continual effort have I earned the right to succeed with this particular skill set. And just because I recognize that I am a decent communicator when it comes to speaking, does not mean I don't recognize that I have room to improve.

On the other hand, I am not a great communicator when it comes to writing. I'm realistic about that. Because I acknowledge that I'm not a great writer, I ask questions, I seek guidance, and I ask for help. Viewing my current skill set through a realistic lens, I give myself the foundation for improvement in my life.

Showing humility is not an opportunity to beat yourself up. In fact, I believe humility and confidence go hand in hand. Both are required to thrive.

With regard to my writing abilities, humility allows me to see my shortcomings. It's confidence, however, that allows me to do something about it. If I didn't have some level of confidence—not in my writing ability itself, but in my ability to learn how to get better at writing—I might never give myself the opportunity to try my hand.

This is why confidence is essential. Most would have you believe that confidence is something to be shunned or put away. I believe confidence is something to be embraced. How many poor souls have never attempted anything great because they're not even confident enough to give it a try?

My oldest son has a hard time with this. This year, he started his third year of football. After the first practice, he came to me with tears in his eyes and said, "Dad, I'm not good at football. I don't know how to throw the ball, I'm not very fast, and I don't understand the rules."

I said, "Son, how many practices have we had this year?"

"One," he said.

I said, "How many games have you played this season?"

"None."

"You haven't earned the right to be as good as you'd like yet," I shared. "But do you remember what you said to me at the beginning of baseball season last year?"

He said, "Yes, I told you I didn't want to play because I wasn't very good at it."

"Right. And how did you feel about the season after it was over?"

"I loved it!" he exclaimed.

"Exactly! Because you learned the game and you got better. Don't you think it's safe to assume you'll experience the same thing in football?"

Of course, this is exactly what happened. He went on to have an incredible year of football and can't wait to play again next year.

You don't need confidence in the skill you're trying to master in order to master it. You need confidence that you can learn the skill you're trying to master. And you do that by drawing on past experiences where you've succeeded.

Humility alone is reserved for those who are too timid, scared, and weak to try anything new. Humility coupled with confidence is a powerful combination for growth, expansion, and sovereignty.

THE MINDSET—I AM OPEN-MINDED AND ALWAYS WILLING TO LEARN

At the end of the day, arrogance, pride, and overconfidence keep you from learning what you need to in order to succeed at home, at work, and in your life in general. You may be deploying an unhealthy level of confidence to display some sort of misguided and perceived power, but when you do, you accomplish the exact opposite.

When you walk around with the attitude that you know it all and that you can't learn anything new, you put yourself in a position of weakness, not a position of strength. You hinder growth, limit expansion, and set yourself up for failure.

To combat the natural tendency we all have to allow our egos to get the better of us, it's imperative we adopt the mindset, "I am a learner." The idea that we are all students in this life gives us the necessary framework and reminder that we aren't required to know it all in any given scenario. If we are to make something of ourselves and more fully serve those we care about, all we have an obligation to do is learn.

When I think about the power of humility and a mind open to new information, I can't help but think about my children. Children are great askers of questions. It's the reason the "Quiet Game" even exists.

Dad, why is the sky blue? Why does he look like that? What is she doing? How fast can a car go? What is your desk made of? Why is carpet soft? Where do babies come from? How old are you? Why does poop stink? The list of questions is endless.

It's fascinating that children have no concern for others' opinion of them. This freedom of judgment from others gives them the leeway to ask any question that could possibly come to mind. In many ways, sovereignty requires the child's mindset: if you don't know, ask.

THE SKILL SET

Be Curious. The foundational skill set to becoming more humble is to be more curious. Falling prey to the trap of arrogance is a dead end. As I've said before, it crushes growth and expansion.

Nowhere has this been more evident than in my evolution as a podcaster. For the first year of podcasting, I would take meticulous notes, write out scripts, and prepare advanced questions. Not that this process isn't helpful, but my objective was merely to appear that I knew what I was doing—that I was a professional.

Unfortunately, the result was interviews that lacked fluidity, passion, and flexibility as I had given no room for the conversation to expand. In many ways, the interviews fell flat because I was more concerned about looking the part than being the part.

Fortunately, I realized this and have since taken an entirely new approach to the way I interview my guests. Now, I come from the perspective of curiosity. I genuinely want to know what my guests are doing, what they're thinking, and how they're producing results in their lives. My questions are much more fluid, the interviews are much more conversational, and both my audience and I gain significantly more value on our own journey to become the men we are meant to be.

You can pretend you know what you're talking about, or you can take the time to learn something new. The former leads to a stalemate; the latter leads to expansion.

Include Others. Humble people include others. Those men who are overly prideful and arrogant have a tendency to believe that they're an island and that they are above anyone else who may simply be along for the ride.

Whether you know it or not, you have not achieved any level of success in your life without the help of someone else. Never overlook that. There are countless men and women who have helped me get to where I am.

When I neglect that fact and fail to remember that most of us are here to accomplish a lot of the same things, I spit in the face of anyone who has helped me along the way. And I'm less likely to have those people and others rally around me in the future.

It is not noble to sit atop the throne by yourself. We live in a time where access to information and amazing people is readily available. Use a team.

CHAPTER 14

INTEGRITY

"We make men without chests and expect from them virtue and enterprise. We laugh at honor and are shocked to find traitors in our midst."

-C. S. Lewis

Let's get something straight, if you can't live your life with integrity, you haven't earned the right to call yourself a man. There's no other way to put it.

Boys lie. Boys don't admit when they are wrong. Boys refuse to fix their mistakes. Boys cover their tracks. Men, however, strive to live their lives with a moral compass. When they mess up, they recognize it quickly and correct it. When they say they'll do something, they do it. Plain and simple. This is what it means to live with integrity.

Any man who lives his life habitually without integrity does great damage to his heart, mind, and soul. Although a man may never be caught in his indiscretion, the consequences of a guilty conscience and a heavy heart are equally, if not more, damaging to a man's freedom and liberty.

I have friends, for example, who have cheated on their spouses. Rather than fess up to their infidelity, they carry the burden of guilt, sorrow, and remorse for years—in some cases, decades—before the weight of that burden becomes unbearable. I can see the torment and fear in these men's eyes as they spend their waking hours consumed with the darkness that festers inside them. The cancer they carry then spreads into their relationship. It enters the heart of a spouse who feels neglected, and it destroys the connection they once had. Their children also feel the effects of their father's guilt as they get pushed to the back burner while their father wrestles with his conscience. In many cases, the feelings of bitterness, animosity, and resentment on both sides of the aisle lead to separation and divorce and further hardens the hearts and minds of the people who once loved each other.

What a shame it takes so long for these men to finally admit their offense. How quickly could the marriage have been salvaged? How much sooner could hearts have been healed? How many resources could have been preserved for more meaningful work? How much good could otherwise have been done?

I realize this may be an extreme example, but regardless of the severity of a man's wrongdoing, the result is always the same: bondage to the dark emotions that consume a man when he's out of alignment with who he wants to be.

That said, we all mess up. It's normal. We are human after all. I've failed to follow my moral compass more than I'd like to admit. But that's not the point. The point is to recognize that we have faltered, do it quickly, and get back our integrity with what we know to be true.

RIGHT AND WRONG

Many people will argue that not all people know what's right or wrong. I call bullshit. Everyone (who's sane) knows what is right and what is wrong. It's the reason the most innocent human beings—children—lie. It's also the reason my two-year-old hides in the corner when he poops his pants. I recognize that may not be a great example, but it highlights the fact that we all know the difference between right and wrong.

If we truly didn't know, we wouldn't try to justify our behavior. My son wouldn't hide in the corner and I wouldn't lie. If we truly didn't know, we'd simply state the facts and drive on. We might even wonder why people were so upset. Consider psychopaths, for example. These are human beings who have little or no conscience. In many cases, when they're caught, there is a complete lack of empathy, sorrow, or remorse for committing what most would consider some horrible atrocities.

Barring an extreme mental disorder, it is safe to assume that we know what's right and wrong. When we know we are about to do something that goes against our moral compass, our hearts start to race, we start to sweat, and a thousand thoughts run through our minds about how we might justify what we're about to do. Those symptoms are indicators that we should not proceed with what we're about to do. I know it's difficult in the moment, considering we might be emotional or desperate, but it's much easier to reevaluate our actions than live with the pain they might cause.

When you willingly proceed with something you know is wrong, you might as well slap the proverbial handcuffs on yourself, because you're about to make yourself a prisoner—a prisoner to another and a prisoner to the destructive power of the mind when you live out of integrity with yourself.

RECTIFY PAST MISTAKES

You may have already submitted yourself to the bondage that comes with your deceit. If that's the case, it isn't too late to do something about it. As I said before, we all mess up. It's in our nature. We fall short. We lie. We cheat. We steal. We take advantage of a situation. We do those things and worse.

The key to unlocking the shackles that keep you bound comes in the form of rectifying the situation—correcting your behavior and making things right. It isn't convenient. It isn't comfortable. It isn't easy.

But then again, neither is living with the pain you've created for yourself. In other words, you can choose your hard. You can place yourself in a difficult situation temporarily and relieve yourself of the burden of your shame. Or you can live with that shame, guilt, and remorse indefinitely. If you choose the path to alleviate your guilt and set the record straight, you'll need to first, own your mistake; second, right the wrong; and third, learn the lesson moving forward.

OWN YOUR MISTAKE

You can never fully liberate yourself from your sorrow if you never fully recognize what you've done wrong and take responsibility for your actions. One without the other isn't adequate. Recognition without responsibility is indifference. Responsibility without recognition is remorselessness.

We've all seen celebrities and athletes who've been caught in scandals. It's painfully obvious that their scripted apologies are a weak attempt at maintaining their status and nothing more. They recognize what they've done is wrong but have not taken responsibility for it.

RIGHT THE WRONG

You cannot fully rectify past mistakes if you aren't willing to right the situation. If you steal from someone, you owe them the cost of what you stole. If you've slandered someone, you need to correct your statements and apologize. If you've taken credit for another man's work, you need to give credit where credit is due.

This may be the most difficult part of making a situation right because it requires you to face the victim of your dishonesty. As challenging as it may be, it's an integral part of the process.

LEARN THE LESSON

If you keep making the same mistake over and over, how remorseful can you be? A man who refuses to learn from his mistakes hasn't fully expressed remorse and/or accepted responsibility. If he did, he wouldn't continue to make the same mistakes again and again.

This is a critical part of the healing process as well. Learning the lesson allows you the opportunity to forgive yourself and become a better man through what would otherwise be only a negative experience. Looking at everything as a lesson is the framework required to make better choices moving forward.

BE A MAN OF YOUR WORD

Equally important to owning up to your mistakes and fixing them is being a man of your word. We all understand this. If you become a man who can't be counted on to do what he says he will, you lose credibility, influence, and ultimately power in your life.

The challenge arises not when we make grand promises and commitments but when we make the seemingly insignificant ones. I've told my oldest son I'll play football with him after work only to "conveniently" forget. I've told my wife I'd walk the dog when I had no intention of ever walking the dog. I've told people I'd show up to help them move when I knew full well I wasn't going to.

Whether we'd like to admit it or not, making a commitment and not living up to that commitment makes liars of men. It doesn't matter what came up. It doesn't matter what excuse you create. Unless you do *exactly* what you said you will, you are a liar. There's no way to sugarcoat it. And every time you lie, a little piece of your soul dies.

You begin to believe that some lies are okay. You rationalize your lies by telling yourself you're busy or your priorities are elsewhere. We fabricate all kinds of wonderful stories designed to give us a pass at being men of integrity.

It's been said that the way we do one thing is the way we do everything. If you lie to your kids about your willingness to help them with their homework, what precedent are you setting in your life for the weight of your words? When you lie about the little things, it isn't long before you lie about the big things.

As I put together a schedule (and as the timeline gets closer) for the release of this book, I've decided to ramp up the number of words I write on a daily basis. Right now, I've committed to writing two thousand words per day. When, for whatever reason, I don't write my two thousand words, I tell myself, "It's okay, I can make them up tomorrow." Then tomorrow comes and goes, and the next day comes and goes. The lies we tell ourselves tend to spiral out of control. In this case, I can justify it by telling myself I'm only a couple thousand words behind. But that couple thousand words may turn into five thousand, then ten thousand, and before long, I may decide to scrap the book altogether.

One of the mistakes I see many men fall prey to is the connection (or lack thereof) with their children. These men are busy with work, for example, and miss little Tommy's baseball game. "He'll understand," they hope. He might. But miss enough games, and Tommy will begin to believe you don't care about him, and, ultimately, he'll lose faith in his father. How powerful can you be if no one believes in you?

Another trap men fall into is doing work less than they're capable of. I once hired a painter to paint my office. He was fairly inexpensive, professional, and friendly. After he finished and left for the day, I came into the office to look around. At first, I was pleased. The color was right, nothing had spilled onto the carpet, the furniture was put back in place, and all seemed well.

Then I looked a little closer. This guy hadn't taped off any of the corners or taken off any of the outlet wall plates. The lines were anything but straight, and every one of my wall plates was covered in blue paint. Did this guy think I wouldn't notice? Or did he just not care?

Either way, it's an integrity issue. Now, he may not have committed to the quality of the work he would do, but I believe it's implied. When I pay a man to do a job, I want it done the right way. But what is "right?" That's subjective. Or is it? Refer back to the section about knowing what is right and what is wrong. We all know when we're shorting ourselves and shorting others.

When you do work less than you're capable of, you rob yourself of the benefits of going the extra mile and maintaining a higher standard for yourself.

The solution to living with integrity is simple: do what you say you're going to do; don't say you'll do something if you're not going to do it.

It really isn't that difficult to understand. I know we may have demands on our time and be experiencing pressure from spouses, coworkers, bosses, etc., but I'd rather give an accurate assessment of what I'll do than lie simply to appease another person.

THE MINDSET—I DO WHAT IS RIGHT AND FIX IT WHEN I'M WRONG

Are you an honorable man or aren't you? I know this might come across as harsh, but integrity is one area of life that's black and white. I know we can all come up with stories and situations where the lines of integrity are blurred. Some situations may even be justified. Does a man lack integrity if he steals a loaf of bread to feed his starving children? The truth? Yes, he does.

I remember an incident when I was asked by my stepfather to fill in and patch a section of grass in our yard. I was tired. I had just

mowed the lawn. I probably had a football game or wrestl·
the night before. So, rather than do the job right, I cut out a piece
of grass from the back of the lawn and simply threw it into the area
that needed to be fixed.

I knew I was in for it when my stepfather decided to come out
and check my work. He walked straight to that patch job and pulled
up the grass. Of course, he noticed the hole that was not filled in.
Rather than get upset, he shared a simple message with me.

He said, "Ryan, I know you're tired. I know you didn't want to
do this job, but being a man of character is about how you behave
and what you do when no one is looking." And he walked off without another word.

I completed the task the right way, and it's a lesson that has stuck
with me since.

With so many people in this world willing to deceive, manipulate, and fraud you, you should be the one person you can count on.
When you lie, cheat, steal, and do work less than you're capable of,
you're not only injuring the people who rely on you, you're defeat-
ing yourself and crippling your chances of Sovereignty.

Being honorable and living with integrity is easy when things
are going well. But that isn't really the test of a man's integrity.
It's how you handle yourself when things are going wrong—when
you're tired, angry, upset, or feeling cheated. During those times,
you will be tempted to lie, cheat, justify, rationalize, and attempt to
fool yourself into taking a pass on integrity. In that hour, decide to
be an honorable man.

THE SKILL SET

Underpromise. It's easy to get excited in the moment. It's easy to
make up a little lie about what you're going to do when you know
a customer has an expectation you know you can't meet. It's easy
to be unrealistic about what you can accomplish.

Whether it's delusion or fear, you must be willing to resist the temptation to promise more than you're capable of delivering. Sure, when you overpromise, your client is going to be happy about it. But when the day of reckoning comes and you haven't completed what you said you would, you're not only going to have an upset client; you're going to have no client at all.

If you know you can't make a deadline, don't say you will. If you know a client's expectations are too high, it's your job to let them know. If you know you won't be able to take your wife out this weekend, or make little Timmy's game, don't lead them on.

And, if the schedule gets moved around or you're a little more efficient than you thought you'd be, you'll have people who are pleasantly surprised—not surprised and pissed.

Fail Fast. As I said before, we all fail from time to time. We make up little white lies. We underestimate how long a project will take. We attempt to appease people by telling them things that aren't true. It happens.

If you are to be a man of integrity, the key is to recognize and learn from these failures quickly. If you refuse to recognize that you messed up, all you're doing is delaying the inevitable— inevitably a client will leave you or you'll get sued or you'll lose the faith of those closest to you.

It's going to happen anyway, so recognize it quickly, own the mess-up as fast as you can, create a solution, and keep driving on.

Men of integrity fix their mistakes fast. Men without integrity dance circles around their failures indefinitely.

CHAPTER 15

CONVICTION

"We should not, like sheep, follow the herd of creatures in front of us, making our way where others go, not where we ought to go."
-Seneca

Having conviction doesn't mean you're loud or insulting. It's interesting to watch grown men act like children, then, when called out on it, recite the words "Zero f**ks given" or "I can do whatever the f**k I want." It's as if the cruder and more disrespectful these guys are, the stronger they feel.

While I can agree that every man has the right to do and say what he wants, a man of genuine conviction doesn't feel the need to do so. A man of conviction doesn't need to prove anything to anyone. He's confident. He's secure. And he's able to act independently of others' opinions, thoughts, and ideas without the need or desire to tell another man he's wrong or "assert" himself in the moment. Frankly, he doesn't care. He knows he's operating with a clear conscience. His mind and heart are free.

Some might consider this indifference. In many ways it is. A man of conviction knows exactly who he is and why he's here, and he's bold in the way he approaches his life. He doesn't care about the opinions of the critics. He cares about living in alignment with who *he* is.

We've all seen what conviction looks like. It may be difficult to quantify, but we've all experienced what happens when a man who is confident walks into a room. He doesn't have to say a thing. He doesn't have to announce he's there. He doesn't feel obliged to make a scene. He simply walks into the room and allows his presence to do the talking. Many would call it the X factor. I call it conviction.

When a man frees himself of the need to be validated or approved by others, he is more able to step into the role he knows he is meant to pursue. Consider how you might skew your thoughts and actions if your highest objective is to be "found worthy" of the people around you.

A man who believes his highest purpose is to win over other people rather than follow his own ambitions robs himself of the sovereignty that comes only with knowing who he is and acting upon that knowledge. This is a component of integrity (see Chapter 14, "Integrity"), which is to say his actions are in line with his beliefs. Manipulating those thoughts, ideas, and actions is another form of deceit—not toward others, but toward yourself.

YOU WILL BE JUDGED

Look, I get it. For a long time, I used to concern myself too much with what others thought of me. I said all the "right" things. I did all the "right" things. My hope was that if I did what I was "supposed" to do, I would succeed. How wrong I was.

What ensued was years of frustration, discontent, and dissatisfaction. The more I tried to make others happy, the more I became unhappy with myself.

We've all experienced it. As Robert Quillen says, "Too many people spend money they haven't earned, to buy things they don't want, to impress people they don't like." But why? Why do we do this to ourselves?

I would argue we make the decisions we make out of a fear of judgment—more specifically, *negative* judgment. We have no problem when people judge us positively. Negative judgment is an entirely different story. And doesn't this play into how we're hard-wired? We, as a species, are constantly striving to move toward pleasure and away from pain. Unfortunately, in order to satisfy this desire, we're willing to lie, cheat, and steal. This is at direct odds with the liberty of our hearts and minds.

I've got news for you. You are going to be judged negatively *regardless* of what you do. You could be preaching love and tolerance for all, and people will come up with something to find fault in.

In a way, you're damned if you do and damned if you don't. So, it's best to do what *you* believe is right and to hell with the critics. If you are to regain control of your heart and mind, you're going to have to come to terms with the fact that you're going to be judged regardless of what you do. Get used to it. It's part of the path.

If we look even deeper, it isn't the judgment we're worried about. We're worried about the *impact* of that judgment. Humans have a deep-seated desire to be accepted and a deep-seated fear of being rejected. One of our greatest primal fears is that we'll be ostracized from the group.

This worry was a legitimate concern for thousands of years. It used to be that, if we became isolated from the group, we faced a very real threat to our existence. We are strong in numbers. We haven't evolved away from this line of thinking, although the threat of rejection isn't nearly as dangerous as it once was. In an effort to keep safe and stay with the tribe, we attempt to fit in, to toe the line, to be accepted.

How do we combat the need to feel like we belong?

First, through an understanding that rejection is no longer life-threatening. At the end of the day, the rejection we may experience is only damaging to our ego, not our lives.

Second, through a healthy level of confidence in yourself and who you are.

CONFIDENCE IS EARNED

One of the most frequently mentioned topics in our Facebook group and conversations is the idea of confidence. It seems to me there is a real lack of confidence in many men today.

What's interesting is that most men who lack confidence somehow feel they're entitled to it—that by their very existence, they have a right to confidence. They don't. Confidence is earned. It's earned through blood, sweat, and tears. It's earned through the display of courage (more in Chapter 19) required to engage in the very activity you lack confidence in.

It's easy to sit on the sideline and observe men who have healthy levels of confidence. We might falsely believe that some men are born with it. I don't believe that's true. What we perceive as confidence in others is either excessive pride and arrogance (refer to Chapter 13) or simply the result of years of pain and discomfort that come with being engaged in the work required to foster it.

Take the *Order of Man* podcast for example. When I set out to launch a podcast nearly three years ago, I had no idea what the hell I was doing. I was nervous. I was anxious. I was lacking confidence. This makes sense; I hadn't earned it yet. But I started it anyway. Fast forward three years. I have plenty of confidence in my ability to host powerful conversations with some incredible people.

It takes me significantly less time to prepare than it used to. The questions I ask are more assertive. The conversations are deeper and more meaningful. Why? Because I have earned the right to those results through the effort of podcasting. As of this writing, I have recorded more than 220 shows without missing a single week!

Guys will ask me:

"Ryan, how do I get more confident with women?" You talk with women.

"How do I get comfortable asking for a promotion?" You ask for a promotion.

"How do I get comfortable in my ability to do _____?" You do _____ more often.

Through courage comes action. Through action comes confidence. Through confidence comes conviction.

SOME OPINIONS COUNT

Knowing that confidence comes through courage begs the question, "Can a man display courage without some level of confidence?" I believe the answer is yes. We all have an ingrained sense of courage that can be fostered and developed into the boost needed to take action.

That said, there are sources of courage beyond our own internal belief system. When my two oldest children were learning to swim, I didn't just throw them in the deep end and say, "Have courage, son!" That would have spelled certain death. No, my wife and I swam with them. We taught them to float. We taught them the strokes. We put them in swim classes.

The same holds true for you when committing to take on a new venture. Sometimes, trial by fire is exactly what's needed. Other times, you need to learn the fundamentals before jumping into the pool.

What's fascinating is, oftentimes the men with the "zero f**ks" mentality I mentioned earlier don't take into consideration the opinions, ideas, experience, and insights of those who might actually have something valuable to share.

When you live your life at a complete disregard for others' opinions, you discount the power of tapping into those who have gone before. The fact is, some opinions actually matter. You're going to have to discern between those that do and those that don't, but if you can properly learn to make that distinction, you'll be much more powerful than those who are oblivious to the expertise of those qualified to share it.

I can't imagine where my financial planning practice and the movement we've created with Order of Man would be without the invaluable guidance and direction of those who have done exactly what I was looking to do. It would have been easy for me to "just do it," only to find out years later I was doing the wrong things.

In reality, my ability to connect with other successful people has given me the validation and, at times, the proverbial kick in the ass I needed to take required action. Never discount the opinions of those who are qualified, in your corner, and want you to succeed. They'll become a powerful source of external motivation, inspiration, and accountability. When combined with an internal drive to do the work you're called to do, they will make you a man of unstoppable conviction.

FINDING YOUR WHY

Accountability to others is overrated. That's an interesting statement, considering I just told you that other people can provide much-needed accountability to get you pointed in the right direction.

That said, accountability to others represents a lower tier of accountability. Although others can provide a much-needed kickstart and a point in the right direction, becoming too dependent on them hinders personal progress and growth.

What happens when the person you relied on, for whatever reason, is no longer there to motivate and inspire you? When that day inevitably presents itself, you'll be left to rely on the person who matters most: yourself. Accountability to yourself represents a higher tier of accountability and one that we would all do well to strive for.

At the end of the day, it boils down to doing what you said you would do *simply because* you said you would do it. But let's face it, life is a challenge. People get sued. People die. The market corrects itself. Technology renders your position obsolete. People get sick. Your kids get into trouble. You get scared. Someone makes a comment that keeps you from moving forward.

It's impossible for you to predict these things, but you can hedge against them. This is the reason we're talking about living a Sovereign life—so that we don't subject ourselves to the mercy of outside sources. The best way to hedge against all that life will throw at you is to understand why you're here and what your purpose is.

In my second interview with Jocko Willink, Navy SEAL commander of the most decorated special forces unit of the Iraqi War, he said, "I'm not afraid of anything I'm doing because I'm doing it for the right reasons."

But who's to say what is right? You are. Yours is the opinion that matters, and it's something only you can define. Finding what is right and what drives you can be an arduous task. We treat our "purpose" or our "why" as some magical thing we'll just happen to stumble upon.

Unfortunately, that's not true. Your "why"—the thing that drives you day in and day out—must, like confidence, be earned. We earn it through acting on the ideas and inspirations that inspire us.

Take the Order of Man for example. When I set out on this journey years ago, I had no idea that I was embarking on what has now become a calling and one of the things I've been placed on this planet to do.

It was simply an idea to start a podcast. So, I started one. Then, it was an idea to start a course. So, I started one. Then, it was an idea to start a mastermind. So, I started one. Then, it was an idea to host live events. So, I started hosting live events. Then, it was an idea to write a book. And I've written one.

You aren't entitled to your why, but you do have the right to earn it. You earn it through listening to that inner voice of inspiration and acting upon it.

THE MINDSET—I OPERATE INDEPENDENTLY OF OTHERS

Making choices free of others' opinions and expectations can be a challenging thing to do. In fact, following rules and social norms has served us well to a degree in the past—especially as we were children attempting to understand how the world works and how we operate in it.

But as with anything, what could be a healthy practice can quickly turn destructive if we refuse to accept that there is a time and place for everything. If you have become so reliant and dependent on others' validation that it's hindered your ability to do the things you know in your heart and mind you should be doing, seeking that approval no longer serves you—it cripples you.

A man of conviction is willing to accept the qualified opinions of others but ultimately makes his own choice and carves his own path. It's not easy when the whole world is telling you to behave one way and you know that isn't the journey for you.

Understanding that you will never escape other people's judgment is the first step in acting as your own agent. From there, it's critical that a man matures and develops his "why" and his confidence through deliberate action.

Everyone has an opinion. Everyone has a thought about the way you should be doing things. Most of this comes from a place of love and care. Some of it doesn't. Either way, no one is going to pay your bills. No one is going to accept the consequences of your choices. You are the one who has to live with your actions—make sure they're *your* actions.

THE SKILL SET

Define Your Purpose. Defining your purpose can be one of the most challenging and rewarding experiences you're likely to face on your journey to Sovereignty. It's not something that happens overnight. It must be fostered and developed over years of the repetitive cycle of reflection, action, and review.

Two things, however, keep many men from living with the level of conviction they're capable of: ignorance and fear.

When I say "ignorance," I'm simply referring to the fact that a lot of men just don't know what they ultimately want to be doing in life. This takes time to find. It takes thoughtfulness. And it takes intentionality.

Here are a few questions to get you started:

What are you doing when time goes the fastest?

What would you be doing with your time if money was not a concern?

What are people asking your advice about?

Where does your mind drift throughout the day?

Answering these questions will help illuminate the path you're meant to walk, but it's not always enough.

More often than not, even when a man knows what he wants, the fear of walking alone holds him back. *What if people mock me? What if someone disagrees with me? What if I lose what I have already built? What if friends turn their back on me?* All those things and more will happen. The greater threat lies not in walking alone, but in never doing what you were meant to do.

Take the Next First Step. So, you're working toward your purpose. You're answering the questions listed above. You know you're going to have to display courage on this chosen path and that you may walk it alone. What do you do now?

Very simply, you take action. That's it. There's no real way to dress it up and make it an easier pill to swallow. You *do* the thing you want to be doing. Yes, you're going to come up with all kinds of excuses designed to keep you safe, comfortable, and conforming with the world around you. Recognize that and *do it anyway.*

I've found it helpful to avoid looking at *all* that has to be done and, instead, ask yourself, "What's the next first step?" Then, do that. Once completed, ask yourself again, "What's the next first step?" Then, do that. Over and over and over again.

This is the only path to building confidence and, in turn, developing the conviction of a Sovereign Man to drive on. When life gets tough, drive on. When you don't feel like doing it, drive on. When people leave you, drive on.

As Theodore Roosevelt said, "Do what you can, where you are, with what you have."

What is your next first step?

CHAPTER 16

SELF-AWARENESS

"No man was ever so much deceived by another as by himself."
-Fulke Greville

Self-awareness is such a buzzword these days. Every self-help guru and motivational speaker throws around the word "self-awareness" as an empty rallying cry to all the wannabe entrepreneurs and enlightened of the world . And, whenever a marketer gets ahold of a word, he completely distorts the meaning of it.

Self-awareness isn't about some misguided or surface-level notion that you should know what you're doing and how it's being perceived by others. Self-awareness is about a deep-seated understanding of *why*—*why* you think the way you think, *why* you believe what you believe, *why* you act the way you do, *why* you get mad, *why* you get sad, and *why* you are exactly where you are today.

Some may even wonder if this information is even necessary. What good does it do to understand why you think the way you do as long as you're producing results? In my experience, a man is significantly more productive and has the power to utilize laser-like focus when he's intentional about the thoughts, beliefs, and experiences that drive him in the first place.

In many ways, self-awareness acts as a gauge to measure how far you've come and how far you have yet to go. Without a clear understanding of the driving beliefs and events in your life, you're left to operate in much the same way you always have.

But when you learn to harness the power of your thoughts, ideas, and emotions, they become a powerful leveraging tool to reclaim your own heart and mind and step into the work of a man.

When my wife and I first started having children, I was lost—as any man would be. I had no idea how a father steps up in his children's lives, and rather than engaging with my firstborn son, I disengaged. Truth be told, I was afraid. I had no idea what the hell I should be doing, and the only experience I had to draw upon was the absence of a father in my life. As a consequence, I distanced myself mentally and emotionally.

It wasn't until I took the time and attention to understand *why* I was distancing myself that I began to understand that the experiences I had as a child helped drive the way I operated as an adult. When we begin to see that past experiences, thoughts, and conversations dictate the way we behave decades later, we give ourselves the power to choose a new way to operate.

OPERATING IN THE DEFAULT

Most of us, however, are operating in a default status. We drive to work the same way. We eat the same food. We listen to the same music. We have sex the same way.

Good, bad, or indifferent, our interactions consist of a few simple scripts we've executed over and over again. They have become our programming—our operating system. The reason that you are experiencing the results in your health, your business, your relationships, and every other facet of life is because the scripts you've been running are producing those results. And even more interesting is that the scripts and subsequent results are predictable.

This is an empowering reality considering the fact that, by adding a new variable to the script or the equation, we can predictably produce a different result. In fact, if you have any desire to achieve a new outcome, you *have to* introduce something new to the equation. It's the only way to change.

Consider the man who's attempting to lose weight and get his health in check. He makes a few changes to his diet, his sleep patterns, his activity level, and his exercise program, and, surprise, surprise, he loses the weight. New variable, new results. Unfortunately, most of the people who do this end up reverting back to their default internal scripts and putting the weight back on.

To affect lasting change, you cannot simply change the external outputs; you have to change the internal inputs. You have to rewrite the programming. And you can't rewrite the programming until you know what the initial programming is in the first place.

To go back to the man who is attempting to make healthier choices in his life, maybe as a child his mother rewarded him with cake and ice cream every time he did something good. Now, he equates eating sweets with a reward for good behavior. Maybe every time he messed up, his dad made him go outside and chop wood. Now, he equates physical exercise with messing up.

The default mode you are currently operating in is not inherently bad. There are plenty of scripts you operate by that produce positive results. The whole point of becoming self-aware is to first, understand the scripts; second, objectively look at the results the scripts are producing; and third, proceed accordingly.

To effectively become more self-aware, there is one simple question I ask myself on a daily basis: "Is this thought serving me or hindering me?"

I had a business mentor once tell me that when he started hiring employees for the first time, he hated it. He believed that good employees were impossible to find, and, given the opportunity, his employees would steal from him every single time. He also subscribed to the idea we've all heard: "If you want it done right, you have to do it yourself."

It wasn't until his business mentor asked where that idea came from that my mentor realized he'd learned that from his father, who, coincidentally enough, had employees who stole from him.

Once he identified the source of his thoughts and actions, he was able to ask, "Is this serving me?" He knew that, to grow his business to the level he wanted, he would need help. He set about learning how to hire employees correctly and implement systems that would limit the opportunities and desire for employees to steal. Armed with this knowledge and action, he now runs a nine-figure business with more than twenty-five employees.

CONJURING UP THE PAST

This story demonstrates the power of revisiting your past. This is not, however, an opportunity for you to dwell on what could have been or how you might have been robbed by your parents, teachers, coaches, counselors, mentors, etc. Conjuring up the past is an opportunity for you to understand yourself and how your thoughts and beliefs came to be.

In addition to asking yourself whether a thought serves you, another powerful question is, "Where does this idea come from?" You could not possibly have a thought without learning that thought from somewhere and/or something. Striving to understand the answer to that question arms you with the knowledge needed to consciously decide whether you still believe that thought is true.

This is the power of being a human being—the ability to change simply because we want to. But you'll never change and, in turn, create a new reality for yourself if you aren't able to examine what drives your thought-making process in the first place.

Unfortunately, most men use the exercise of looking into the past as an opportunity to judge themselves. We should not, however, judge ourselves, only the action, experience, and/or encounter that helped drive us to become who we are today. This is a big distinction.

It would be very easy for a man who has gained too much weight to consider himself a fat, lazy slob. Let's revisit the question I proposed earlier: "Does this thought serve him?" No, it hinders him and potentially keeps him from moving forward. After all, he has resigned himself to being a fat, lazy slob. He may *have* fat. He may *act* lazy. He may *be* sloppy. He is not, however, a fat, lazy slob unless he chooses to define himself that way. Revisiting the past is an exercise in examining what has transpired so you can objectively decide whether it's serving you and your ambitions.

EMOTIONS

One of the hardest things for a man to overcome on his journey to become self-aware is the pressure of society regarding what a man *should* and *shouldn't* be. Let's be honest, much of what you are reading in this book could be considered the same. I'm confident that, armed with the knowledge shared here, you can decide for yourself.

That said, when you cling too tightly to what I or anyone else thinks, you limit your potential to make a life *you* are excited about. And one of the biggest hurdles we face is society's pressure to put away our emotions.

It's not just sorrow and fear we're asked to hide. It's anger. It's jealousy. It's rage. We're told that a *real* man doesn't display his emotions. I disagree. I think the display of emotions is a human condition, for woman *and* men.

I hear from men every single day who ask how they can temper their anger or how they can overcome the sorrow they may be experiencing. In many ways, I think this is a major contributor to depression and, ultimately, suicide in men.

A man should not be required to hide his emotions in order to be considered a real man. But I do think a man would be well-served to *understand* his emotions. If you're pissed off because you got passed up for a promotion, good. Maybe that anger will drive you to do the work required to secure the next one. If you're sad that your wife left you, good. Maybe you'll wake the hell up and go to work on yourself so you can salvage the marriage. If you're feeling down on yourself because you yelled at your kid, good. Now you can apologize and learn from your mistake.

Emotions aren't bad, regardless of what people are telling you. Anger, greed, jealousy, rage, joy, sorrow, love, hate—all of them are good. All of them are there to serve you. When you attempt to hide them, you negate the power the spectrum of emotions has to tell you what's working in your life and what isn't.

I'd have you consider that when you tell yourself you *shouldn't* cry, you've subscribed to a lie. You *should* cry and you should strive to *understand* why you're crying. When you tell yourself you shouldn't be so angry, you're overlooking a tool to help you on your journey to become a Sovereign Man. You should be angry and you should strive to *understand* why you're angry.

The key to controlling your emotions is not to hide them, it's to *understand* and *learn* from them.

THE MINDSET—I UNDERSTAND WHO I AM

The journey of self-awareness and self-discovery will not happen overnight. It will take years to master and develop. But once you learn where your thoughts and ideas come from, what experiences make you think and act the way you do, and what your emotions are trying to teach you, you make yourself the master of yourself.

See, most men wander around all day, every day without a clear understanding of who they are. I know how frustrating this can be. For a long time, I could not understand why I felt like there was something missing from my life. I knew I was destined for more—in my business, my health, my relationships, and my life. For years, I walked around as a shell of the man I knew I was meant to be. I would see people succeed and be pissed off that I wasn't succeeding. I allowed my emotions to control my life because I refused to see them for what they are. I wallowed in my ignorance because I believed I could not fully express what I was experiencing.

Through years of study, research, and experimentation, I've found that continually striving to find who you really are and what really makes you tick is the most liberating journey you can take. For the first time in my life, I am free from my expectations because I have a firm understanding of who I am, and, more importantly, I take the actions those conclusions bring me to.

Without an understanding of who he is and why he is the way he is, a man will never truly be sovereign. Consciously or unconsciously, he will always subject himself to the expectations of others and himself. The journey to sovereignty will never be complete until a man understands who he truly is and steps into it with all his heart and mind.

THE SKILL SET

Margin. The single biggest hurdle to becoming more self-aware is our constraint of time. Look, I get it, as men we have a lot of responsibilities and obligations. There just doesn't seem to be enough time in the day to do all we need to get done, let alone adding time to just *sit and think.*

But if we have any hope of becoming more self-aware, intentional, and deliberate about our lives, creating the margin to ask ourselves powerful questions is an absolute necessity.

Whether it's some form of meditation, hiking outdoors, participating in your hobby of choice, or just sitting quietly somewhere, allowing yourself uninterrupted time to think is a pivotal move on your journey to become a Sovereign Man.

I personally would suggest that you get out of bed thirty minutes early. This is a great time to reflect on your life and what you want out of it. Most of the family won't be out of bed, it will be quiet, and you won't get bogged down with distractions like e-mail and phone calls.

Participating in morning reflection isn't enough, however. It wasn't until I added some time in the evening that I really began to see the results of understanding who I am and what makes me operate the way I do. I would suggest you make it a goal to complete your work a half hour before you normally do and use the remaining thirty minutes as a time to unwind, destress, and reflect. Not only is this a great way to cap your day, but it will help you be more aware of what you'd like to get done the following day.

Outside of a morning and evening routine, reflection throughout the day is crucial. If you notice you're getting upset over something, don't freak out and lose your cool. Simply ask yourself, "Does this serve me?" and "Where does this anger, joy, sorrow, frustration, etc. come from?" Armed with the answers to these questions, you create the bedrock for understanding who you are and recapturing control of your thoughts, ideas, and emotions.

Replace the Script. Once you have the practice of margin down and begin to see where everything you think, believe, and feel comes from, you have two choices: stay the course or change the path.

There's nothing wrong with answering the two questions I posed earlier and deciding *consciously* that the beliefs do, in fact, serve you, then *choosing* to remain in the default. This is the ultimate goal—to have such a clear understanding of who we are and the ability to act upon it that it no longer requires focus and attention to do it. In other words, aligning your beliefs with your actions has become habitual.

That said, if you do decide to change courses, you're going to have to replace the scripts and programming you've been operating by all your life. If, for example, you smoke cigarettes and you have a clear understanding of where this comes from, you can now change what you tell yourself about the act of smoking. Whether it's cigarettes, alcohol, rage, or any number of things you recognize as not serving you, never underestimate the mind's ability to change. We call this neuroplasticity, which is the brain's ability to form and reorganize synaptic connections.

This, of course, doesn't happen overnight, but through consistent reflection, margin, and replacing the scripts you run your life by, you can literally rewire the brain to serve you more effectively.

There was a time when I was drinking up to two energy drinks per day. I decided that these drinks did not serve me and replaced the script I was telling myself about the consumption of these drinks. Believe it or not, I would repeat the phrase, "Healthy people do not drink energy drinks." Whether it's true or not is irrelevant. I had such a deep desire to be healthy that I would do whatever it took to get there, including eliminating energy drinks from my diet. It took a little time, but it was as simple as that.

I realize that may be a small example, but I see results from this skill set on a daily basis. Men are quitting cigarettes, going to the gym, reducing their rage, connecting with their spouses, forging new bonds with their children, budgeting, starting businesses, asking for promotions, and so much more simply by the power of the inputs into their brains—their scripts.

What you tell yourself is powerful—make sure it's serving you.

CHAPTER 17

DISCIPLINE

"There are two freedoms—the false, where a man is free to do what he likes; the true, where he is free to do what he ought."
-Charles Kingsley

If there's one foundational skill that unlocks the key to satisfaction, fulfillment, and contentment in your life, it's discipline. And discipline is a choice. It's something that can be developed. Sure, there may be those who were born with the predisposition or the personality to be more disciplined, but that doesn't, for one second, mean that a man who has lacked discipline in the past cannot learn to develop and harness the power that comes from maintaining action despite his feelings or any outside circumstances.

The only problem with discipline is that no one wants to actually be disciplined. We're more interested in maximum results with minimal effort, and while there is validity to that desire, it does not produce long-term results consistently. This is why discipline is so critical on your journey to take control of your heart and mind. To achieve *lasting, predictable results*, day in and day out, a man must exhibit discipline and dedication to the small actions that produce the big results.

Consider the professional baseball player. He's at the pinnacle of his career. It's likely he's been playing baseball for two to three decades or longer. He probably learned to swing a bat when he was two. In other words, he's the best. He's a master at his craft. He knows the mechanics. He knows the physics. He has the technique of swinging the bat dedicated and locked into muscle memory. And yet, this is the man who still swings off the same rudimentary tool my four-year-old uses to learn the game—the tee.

The professional athlete who still uses a tee and still takes batting practice every single day (although obviously he knows how to hit a baseball) is the man who understands what it takes to succeed at the highest level: discipline.

See, it's easy to look in from the outside at the man who seems to posses some special gift or a certain secret we have yet to find for ourselves, and think, "Isn't he lucky? I wish I was as lucky as he is," or "Wouldn't it be nice to be an overnight success like him?"

We all want to hit it big. We all want things to go our way. We all want the quick hit, the quick fix, and the home run. Look, I get it, the home run is sexy. The singles and doubles required to win consistently are not. When we, however, subscribe to the notion that a man just got lucky or just happened to be in the right place at the right time, we discount the virtue of discipline. Do successful people get lucky? Sure. But that's the exception, not the rule.

You're going to get lucky one day. You're going to hit the lotto. The attractive woman you've had your eye on is going to talk with you. Someone is going to quit and you're, by default, the one who will land the promotion. A big client will call you unexpectedly and out of the blue. It's going to happen. And while it's nice when it does, don't get used to it. *Every* man gets lucky and wins big from time to time. The Sovereign Man knows how to win big consistently through the practice of discipline.

UNREALISTIC EXPECTIONS

There's a hurdle to developing and maintaining discipline. And this hurdle is what keeps most men from achieving all they desire in their relationships, their businesses, their health, and their life. The hurdle is an unreasonable expectation of what it will take to win. Most of us, for whatever reason, seem to overestimate our abilities and underestimate the amount of work it will take to win on any front.

Because we set false expectations, we quit *way* too soon. We bounce around from idea to idea, job to job, workout program to workout program, then have the audacity to ask why we can't seem to get ahead.

You can't get ahead because you restart every six months! Is it really that hard to figure out? You aren't entitled to results regardless of how much you think you *deserve* them. You deserve the results of your consistent effort (discipline), no more, no less.

When I launched my first podcast in the winter of 2014, I got so down on myself because I wasn't seeing the results I had hoped for. I quit after twenty episodes. Twenty episodes! That's not even getting started.

I regrouped and talked with successful podcasters about what it would take to run a large podcast. All of them agreed that it required a minimum of one year of consistent effort.

When I launched Order of Man in the spring of 2015, I committed to doing a podcast every week for at least two years. Two and a half years later, *I have not missed a single week* for over 140 weeks. Guess what? I run a very large podcast that consistently ranks in the top fifty in all the world in multiple categories. This isn't a surprise. It's the result of calculated, ruthless discipline.

When you stop focusing so much on what you want and, instead, focus on what it will take to have it, you put yourself in the right mindset to reach your objectives. In essence, you have to find a way to strip away the expectation of results and have faith that the actions, over time, will get you there.

Once you understand that you'll need to engage in consistent action to reach a desired outcome, you'll need to start identifying hurdles that will come up. And they will. I can't think of one journey I've ever embarked on that went exactly according to plan.

Just this week, I finished a hunt in Texas. The night before the hunt was over, I thought, "Man, this went pretty well. I bagged two bucks. So did my friend. No one got themselves shot. And we had some great times." That night, we got food poisoning.

It's part of the deal. Things are going to go wrong. Understand that, build in some contingency plans, and decide right now to drive on anyway.

As Seneca says, "The man who has anticipated the coming of troubles takes away their power when they arrive."

DO IT ANYWAY

Not only are you going to run into unknowable outside hurdles and barriers on your journey to become more disciplined, but you're going to, at times, get in your own way. You're going to let the way you *feel* dictate the way you behave.

I understand. When the alarm goes off at five every morning, I don't always feel like going to the gym. When I get into the office in the morning, I don't always feel like making follow-up calls and e-mails. When I sit down in front of my computer, I don't always feel like writing the words to the book.

But the way I feel about doing something I've already committed to doing has no relevance to my actually doing it. I am in charge of my emotions, not the other way around. And so are you.

As I illustrated in the previous chapter, your emotions are simply indicators. You can allow them to steer your life or you can take them into consideration and make a conscious choice of what to do next.

Sure, you can make plans and create contingencies. You can set realistic expectations and remove potential barriers to your getting the job done. But even with all that planning, there are going to be events and circumstances that have the potential to derail you, including those nagging little voices that say, "Sleep in just a little longer. You can make those calls later. You'll have plenty of time to write tomorrow."

Do not listen to those voices. Bear down and drive on. Demonstrate a little willpower. Those voices shut up when you tell them to and commit yourself to the cause. As with any skill, willpower can be developed. Not by reading a book about willpower. Not by talking to people about how to be stronger. Not by coming up with a bunch of tricks and hacks to make things easier. You build willpower by exhibiting willpower. Plain and simple. The more you do it, the stronger you become.

I could write a whole book on how to build discipline, but the truth is, the topic doesn't warrant an entire book. Developing discipline is as simple as doing the things you've committed to regardless of whether you want to.

THE MINDSET—I AM RELENTLESS IN THE PURSUIT OF MY OBJECTIVES

No man ever achieved anything great without a relentless pursuit toward greatness. It's not always easy. It doesn't always go smoothly. The battle for your sovereignty gets ugly at times. But unless you can develop the virtue of discipline, you will never be in control of your heart and mind.

The man who neglects discipline in exchange for a short-term gain or to indulge in his vice of choice subjects himself to the vice itself.

Only through the relentless pursuit of our objectives do we rip ourselves away from the very comfortable status quo that has secretly enslaved our hearts and minds. It's all an illusion. What we think is freeing is anything but. The man who is "free" to get himself out of bed later than he knows he should loses valuable time in his day to work toward his goals. The man who is "free" to eat like shit subjects himself to weight gain, illness, and disease. The man who is "free" to screw off at work gets passed over for the promotion time and time again. The man who is "free" to spend his money on anything and everything he feels inclined to purchase gives himself to debt and poverty.

There is only one true way to freedom: discipline.

Aristotle understood this thousands of years ago when he said, "Through discipline comes freedom."

Jocko Willink, arguably one of the most disciplined and successful warriors of our time, understands this when he says, "Discipline equals freedom."

If you want the freedom to get maximum results out of your day, you're going to have to subject yourself to getting up early. If you want the freedom that comes with a long and relatively illness-free life, you have to subject yourself to the discipline of diet and exercise. If you want the freedom that comes with career advancement, you're going to have to subject yourself to the grinding work it takes to achieve it. If you want the freedom that comes with building enormous sums of money, you're going to have to subject yourself to tracking income and expenses and investing wisely.

In other words, choose your free. Will you choose to be free to do what you feel like doing at the risk of the bondage that comes in the end? Or do you want to subject yourself to the discipline required now to achieve ultimate and lasting freedom?

If you choose the latter, you must become relentless in the pursuit of your objectives.

THE SKILL SET

Break It Down. The word "discipline" conjures up thoughts of difficulty. Many of us have come to the conclusion that for something to count, it has to be difficult. Just because exercising discipline will be tough from time to time does not mean that is has to be.

If you can find ways to simplify and make the process easier and/or more obtainable, you'll have a huge advantage over those who feel like they have to grind their way through it.

Take the process of writing this book, for example. It would be easy to focus on the completion of my book, but it's a daunting idea (especially when you're just getting started). Instead of focusing on completing my book, I've decided to break down the process of writing a book into the daily action of writing one thousand words per day.

One thousand words written per day is not a lot of words to write and usually takes me an hour or so. Considering my schedule, this isn't all that challenging, but, again, who said it had to be?

Compounded over two months, the book is completely written, and I can move on to my next objective. Breaking down a big goal into smaller, more manageable actions has helped me maintain the course, especially when I didn't feel like it. And that is the definition of discipline.

Plant Your Flag. One of the biggest hurdles to becoming more disciplined is moving away from the "short game" and into the "long game." This is also the mark of a mature man. Most guys are after immediate results. As I mentioned earlier, they want the home run. They want the unexpected opportunity for the promotion. The want the beach body for the cruise coming up in two months. They want to stumble upon the girl of their dreams. They want a quick buy-out for the app they just developed. While these things all happen from time to time, you'd be better off not banking on the quick hit.

Instead, and to develop more discipline and the sovereignty that comes with it, you'd be better off planting your flag for the way you're going to live your *life*, not just the next two or three months.

When you set realistic expectations about what and how long it will take to succeed, you free yourself from having to swing for the fences to get on the scoreboard.

If you take the "plant your flag" approach, you can do what you *know* you need to do regardless of how you feel about it and regardless of what outside factors may be stacked against you. In a way, you're letting those chips fall where they may because you're not focusing on the immediate results as much as the actions that ultimately produce the results.

In addition, when you play the long game by executing every single day, you put yourself in the perfect position to capture the opportunities that will inevitably present themselves. I can't help but wonder how many amazing opportunities men have missed simply because they haven't been ready to receive them.

What most men recognize as luck, the Sovereign Man recognizes as a long-term commitment to a disciplined life.

CHAPTER 18

MASTERY

"The power of a man increases steadily by continuance in one direction. He becomes acquainted with the resistances, and with his own tools; increases his skill and strength and learns the favorable moments and favorable accidents."
-Ralph Waldo Emerson

When I was playing baseball in high school, one of my coaches, Matt Labrum, would constantly remind us, "You're only as good as your last at bat." We were a pretty good team. We took regionals my junior year and placed fourth in state, and, in my senior year, we took second in regionals. Unfortunately, we let this go to our heads at times and forgot that, although we were good, we had plenty more to learn.

I've seen it time and time again in myself and in countless men. We finally reach some objective we've been working hard at tackling. Once we hit it, we coast, we take it easy, we rest on our laurels. It seems to me that there are a lot of men who are comfortable with mediocrity. While I can understand that some men are more ambitious than others (or have differing priorities), there is *always* something to be mastered.

I can hear the naysayers now: "Ryan, you don't have to be the best at everything. Sometimes it's a hobby. Sometimes it's just for enjoyment." Look, I get it. Not everything has to be a competition to be the best. I enjoy playing catch with my children. I don't for one second believe I'm ever going to be a professional baseball player at the highest level, but you can be damn sure I will strive to be the best at playing catch with my kids.

Mastery isn't about competition with others; it's about competition with yourself. Are you a better man today than you were yesterday? If not, you're not only stagnant, you're falling behind. There is no maintenance plan here. You're either expanding or contracting.

When a man decides to take his foot off the gas, the natural friction of life causes him to slow before he comes to a halt altogether. I hear from men every day who have lost their ambition, purpose, focus, clarity, and drive. What makes it worse is they don't even know why. It's hard to get something back if you don't know what you're missing.

I'd submit that, if you're experiencing these types of feelings in your own life, you've neglected the notion of mastery. You've stopped trying. Maybe you think your work is unfulfilling. Maybe you feel as if you're being stymied by others. Maybe you feel you've reached the highest pinnacle you can reach. For whatever reason, you've stopped trying. You've stopped working to become a master.

But isn't becoming a master a huge part of what being a man is all about? After all, if you can't produce the desired and needed results in your life and the lives of those you care about, what good is it having you around? Now, some may hear that and think it's too harsh and that some men can't handle that. I call bullshit. If you are feeling stuck, you don't need to be coddled. You need to be jerked back into the reality that your "best" may not be good enough. But it's okay. Once you realize that, you can get better. You can become a master.

THERE IS NO ARRIVAL

Here's the first realization you need to understand: there is no arrival. There is no final destination. No glorious state of being where the clouds part and the angels sing, "Hallelujah, you've made it." I know that may not sound very empowering, considering that most men work better when they know what they're working toward.

But let's break this down a little bit and make a distinction. There are going to be projects, jobs, encounters, relationships, and experiences that are going to end. In fact, most of what we deal with on a daily basis is, by design, supposed to end.

What I'm referring to when I say there is no arrival is that you, as a man, will *never* reach your full potential. What does "full potential" even mean? I know we like to talk about it, but I sincerely believe it is impossible. Your potential as a man is a moving target. Once you think you're there, you can plainly see you're capable of so much more.

At first glance that may be a very frustrating idea. If you'll never reach your full potential, what's the point of even trying? But if you think about this on a deeper level, you'll see, if you know there is no state of being where you become your best, you give yourself permission to enjoy the ride you're currently on.

When we spend our entire lives adhering to the notion that there is some final destination for ourselves or, worse, we compare ourselves to where other people are, we become consumed with chasing something that does not exist. If you're chasing something that isn't real, all you end up doing is spinning in circles and not getting anywhere.

Even the thought of mastery can be an elusive target. Does complete mastery even exist? With the advancement in technology and medicine, things that were once impossible are entirely possible today, and even more so in the future. I don't, however, consider mastery an objective. I consider mastery a path—a journey to see how good we can actually become. And isn't that more exciting anyway?

Whether you're sweeping floors and cleaning toilets as a janitor or running a Fortune 500 company, understanding that there is no arrival should fill you with optimism, as there is no limit on what you can ultimately achieve.

ACT LIKE YOU'VE DONE IT BEFORE; ACT LIKE YOU'LL DO IT AGAIN

The same coach I referenced earlier, Matt Labrum, would tell us after celebrating a big win, "Act like you've done it before; act like you'll do it again."

It's great to celebrate your victories. You've earned them. But if you ever begin to believe you've reached as high as you're going to reach, you strip away the power you have to take it to the next level.

We often get so consumed with celebration that we forget, as I stated earlier, there is no final destination. A momentary win is just a stop on your journey to do and be more. Sure, you landed the big sale, but can you do it again?

Sure, you got the girl, but can you keep her?

Sure, you used to run a six-minute mile, but can you do it today?

Unfortunately, too many men wrap up their identity in winning instead of mastery. Insisting on the win at all costs is extremely damaging. If the win becomes more important to you than the experience and learning opportunity, you'll do and say anything to come out ahead. Taken to an unhealthy level, you'll jeopardize your integrity, conscience, and sovereignty just to be crowned the victor.

Don't get me wrong, winning is critical. It's the reason we keep score. It's the reason you're in business. It's the reason you have a scale in your bathroom. At a healthy level, competition can drive a man to push harder than he ever has and to ensure he's practicing for the day it counts. In other words, competition can drive a man to do the work to become a master. But taken to the extreme, he may get so wrapped up in the desire to win, he forgets the work he did to get himself there.

This is why we see athletes who score a touchdown and, instead of celebrating with the men who helped them score, run away from them and bask in all the glory they didn't earn on their own.

A Sovereign Man doesn't have the desire to celebrate needlessly. He keeps his cool; he keeps his composure. He's been here before and he knows he'll be here again. So, rather than make himself look like a fool, he runs to his team, congratulates them for their success, then goes to work reviewing the game film so he can duplicate the results and do it even better next time.

THE MINDSET—I LEARN FROM MY VICTORIES AND FAILURES AND CONTINUE TO GROW

If a man can't learn from *all* he experiences, he will never grow. Unfortunately, I've seen too many men allow both victory and defeat to get the better of them.

Victory can easily get to a man's head if he has no ambition to become a master. Whether he's born with some natural gift and ability or he's worked his ass off to get to where he is, winning may become the ultimate prize, and, therefore, it becomes enough.

Mastery, however, is a tier above winning. While a man may be able to win, a master never settles for it. He knows he can always get better regardless of the ultimate score. When a man who wins decides it's enough for him, he robs himself of potential growth and cuts off any path of learning something new and being exposed to new opportunities. In a way, he allows his success to cripple him because he believes he's already the best; therefore, there is nothing else to be learned or done.

Winning is not enough to a master. You may be able to outperform another, but do you have the capacity to get better than *you* once were?

I've seen failure cripple a man, too. Many men frame failure as an ultimate defeat. We have been led to believe that failure should be avoided at all costs. The only way to completely avoid failure is never to try. So men sit on the sideline, they take it easy, they do just enough to get the job done, and they never strive for more.

Many men are so afraid of failure that they never give themselves the chance to succeed. Most men know this and yet they still have a difficult time overcoming the fear of loss and rejection. The master, however, recognizes failure for what it actually is—not the end, but the beginning of something new.

You got rejected. What will you do differently next time?

You were passed over for the promotion. How will you exert yourself moving forward?

Your business crashed and burned. What did you learn?

Your diet didn't stick. How can you change it?

You went through a divorce. What inadequacies can you shore up?

Failure isn't losing. It's feedback. You found out what didn't work so you can take that real-world feedback and improve your odds next time. People often ask what about my past do I regret or what would I do differently. While I can understand they're looking to learn a lesson of their own before they make their own mistakes, I can't answer that question. All my mistakes and failures have been valuable lessons on my own journey to become a master. Without the mistakes, I would not be the man I am today.

We all have lessons to learn. You're going to learn them at some point. You might as well mess up, learn them quickly, and give yourself permission to do things differently next time. And, trust me, there will be a next time.

Winners plateau. Losers quit. Masters never stop.

THE SKILL SET

Do Less, Master More. In a world that demands more and more of us, I would argue that less actually can be more. We've all heard the adage, "Jack of all trades, master of none." It's true. The more you do, the less effective you become.

It is tempting to do more than you're capable of doing well. Not only do we receive the notoriety and praise of being a man who will always do what is expected of him, but it feels good to do it all. As a high-achieving man, you *want* to do more. It's a test. It's a challenge. It's a thrill. It's exciting. But it doesn't last. Attempting to do it all is betting on a house of cards. It looks great, but it will eventually come crashing down. When it does, the fallout can be devastating.

I've seen men burn out, freak out, and check out because they can't handle the mental, physical, and emotional toll of doing it all for a sustained period of time. No one can. If you think you're the exception to that rule, it may be your ego talking (go back and read Chapter 13).

Learn to let go of the things that don't matter so you can remain hyper-focused on the things that do. Take inventory of your life right now. What are you doing that you shouldn't be? What are you doing that is costing you too much time and money? What are you doing that you don't even enjoy? Once you know what those things are, nix them from your life, or, if they have to get done, delegate them to someone who can do them much more efficiently than you can.

A few things you ought to consider eliminating or delegating are: taxes, yard work, vehicle maintenance, payroll, investment research, unnecessary meetings, e-mails, phone calls, running errands, cleaning your house, home repairs, etc.

You may be fully capable of handling these things on your own, but just because you *can* doesn't mean you *should.* Stop being so-so at everything and get exceptional at a few things.

Permission to Experiment. At some point, you're going to need to give yourself permission to mess up. But rather than looking at it as messing up, let's reframe it as experimentation.

No one wants to mess up. Think back to when you were a child. You got in trouble for messing up. You still do. When you mess up at work, your boss fires you. When you mess up at home, your wife gives you the cold shoulder. When you mess up while driving, you get a ticket.

On the other hand, everyone likes to experiment. When I was a kid, I would climb up on my roof and throw off G.I. Joes with napkins tied to them to see if they would parachute. Even now, I like to experiment: books, toys, firearms, exercise equipment, workouts, food, etc.

Please understand me, some experiments will get you killed. Don't do them. (I can't believe I even have to say this, but I'm sure someone will do something stupid and say, "Well, Ryan said to experiment.")

As long as it's legal, moral, ethical, and won't get you killed, get after it. Reframing the idea of trying new things as an experiment gives you the permission to do something you may not normally do. Not only that, but the process of experimentation allows you to try a different approach with things that have always been done a certain way. It's these differences in the way people approach work, family life, cancer research, expertise, nutrition, etc., that completely revolutionize the way things are done. What is now common knowledge was, at one point, just a theory put to the test.

Experimenting in your life also helps you overcome flat-lining or plateauing on your quest to improve. When you approach your life the way a scientist approaches his research, you allow yourself room to test variables to look for efficiencies in the way you live and operate.

If you let fear dictate what you will and won't do, you'll never grow. If you look at success as the final destination, you'll cut yourself short of what you could have otherwise done. But if you give yourself permission to develop through testing your theories, you will become a master.

CHAPTER 19

COURAGE

"A man without courage is to me the most despicable thing under the sun, a travesty on the whole scheme of creation."
-Jack London

Everything we've talked about up to this point, all of it, really doesn't mean a damn thing if you have an inability to learn and develop the last virtue I want to address with you on your way to sovereignty: courage.

All you've ever read and all you've ever listened to and all you've ever consumed is completely wasted if you can't actually take that information and do the work required to produce the result you're after.

I've never met a single man who didn't have some vision for the future and some idea of a new reality he wanted to create for himself. But I've met plenty of men who lacked the intestinal fortitude to act on those ideas. What a sad truth. How much better would your life be if you had the balls to do what you know you should be doing? How much better off would your family be? How much stronger would the community in which you live be? How much more profitable would your business be?

You can't answer those questions unless (and this is a big unless) you're willing to see if what you've thought so much about will play out the way you think it will. There's absolutely no way to know unless you do it.

But this is where we get hung up. It seems to me that many of us are less concerned with acting courageously than we are with not looking foolish. In a sad way, most of us are playing the game of life not to lose.

Prior to army basic training, I received advice from some of the men in the section I would be working with after basic. Among their advice to survive was, "Don't stand out." I was directed by them to get lost in the crowd. Don't draw attention to myself. Don't fall behind. Don't get out ahead. I didn't know any better, so I went with it. And it worked.

But the more I think about it, the more I realize how horrible this advice actually is. What may have worked for a period of four months certainly isn't any way to live a life worth living. Unfortunately, we see this all the time. You don't share your idea in the board meeting because, "What if the boss doesn't like it?" You don't ask the girl out because, "What if she rejects me?" We don't ask for feedback because, "What if someone criticizes me?"

Hell, I battled this as I wrote the book. I asked myself if I should even write it, knowing that some will reject what I have to say. The reality is that they will. The safe bet would be not to write the book and therefore spare myself the criticism I'm bound to face. But I'm not playing not to lose; I'm playing to win.

How do you play? Do you dive in headfirst or do you fall back when an opportunity presents itself?

After all, if you don't share your ideas, no one will laugh at them. If you don't ask her out, she can't reject you. If you don't ask for feedback, you won't be criticized. You'll be safe. But you'll be trapped.

LEGACY

Understanding that we're here on this spinning rock for a very short time should fill you with a sense of urgency. If it doesn't, I'm not sure what else can be said. You and I are working against a clock. Unlike in a sporting event, however, we don't know when that time will be up. That being the case, it's critical that we make the most of every single minute we do have. Too often we don't. We delay. We coast. We procrastinate.

I can't even begin to tell you how many men ask me how to overcome procrastination. I know it's a real challenge, but it's only a challenge because you believe you have more time than you potentially do. If, for example, you have seventy-two hours to complete a critical assignment, it will take you seventy-two hours to complete. If, however, you have the same assignment due in twenty-four hours, you'll find a way to get it done in twenty-four hours. Same assignment. Same requirements. But it will take you significantly less time. How can this be? In the second scenario, you don't have time to plan, strategize, work out all the angles and potential pitfalls. You only have time to get to work. And work is what gets the job done. This is known as Parkinson's Law: works expands so as to fill the time available for its completion.

Knowing that we often work slower than we're capable of reduces our need for courage—that is, to act in spite of fear and potential failure. When we have more time, we lie, we make excuses, we rationalize, and we stall. By shortening the time allotted, we strip away our natural tendency to drag our feet and give ourselves permission to focus on only the most important tasks—the ones that will actually produce the meaningful results we're after for ourselves and those under our care.

When I recognize that what I do with my time here matters to me and to those who look to me, I reduce my ability to sabotage myself. There's a great scene in the movie *Gladiator* where Maximus attempts to rally his troops before a battle. He says, "Brothers, what we do in life echoes in eternity."

Whether you believe in an afterlife or not, the fact remains, what you do with your limited time here matters. It's your legacy. What will your legacy be? Will it be one of mediocre results driven by a man who was too afraid to do something great? Or will it be one of victory led by a man who was afraid but displayed courage in the face of that fear and showed up fully for himself, his family, and his community?

FEAR OF THE UNKNOWN

One of the most potentially destructive thoughts we have is "What if?" What if this goes wrong? What if this happens? What if that happens? What if someone mocks me? What if I fail? What if I lose my money? What if I lose credibility? What if I lose my friends?

The fact is, we're wired to stay alive, so we're in constant search of the factors that pose a threat to our well-being. But with the advancement of technology, medication, and civility, there are very few things that actually place anything, including our lives, in any real danger. Still, we cannot seem to overcome the plaguing thought of loss to ourselves, our tribe, or our livelihood.

Fortunately, there's a very simple solution to the "What-If Game." Find out. It really is that simple. Most of us live in ignorance about the things that scare us. We conjure up fanciful stories of death and destruction should we display any level of courage to take a new path and put ourselves out into the world. But they're just that—fanciful stories. They're not real. Seneca says, "We are more often frightened than hurt; and we suffer more from imagination than from reality."

I know this is true of me. I can't even begin to count how many times I've started something new I've been afraid of only to realize it wasn't nearly as bad as I'd played it out to be in my mind. Until you're capable of acting, even to the smallest degree, you will remain trapped in a false reality you've created for yourself. Don't you want to know? Don't you want to find out how it really is? Don't you want to unplug from the "matrix?" Unfortunately, many men would rather live in delusion and produce less than they're capable of than face the scary reality that they've limited themselves to less than what's possible.

But here's the deal. Just because you take a peek—and that's all I'm asking you to do right now—at what's behind the curtain, doesn't mean you can't drop the curtain again. I have a feeling you won't, because what you'll find isn't nearly as scary as what you made it out to be in your mind.

Ignorance is only bliss until you realize you're not happy and you can't quite figure out why. I know why you're not happy. Because you're behaving like a boy.

Boys believe in dragons, but they also believe in their capability of slaying them. Somewhere along the way, however, they lose the belief that they can face the dragon and win. Rather than risk the damage to their ego, they place the dragon on a pedestal on which he doesn't belong. "It's too big," the boy says. "It's too scary; it's too dangerous." Bullshit. The boy doesn't even know what's there anymore because he doesn't have the guts to look at the imaginary monster he's created.

I challenge you—maybe for the first time in years or in decades or in your life—to take a look. It's not as scary as you imagine it to be.

THE MINDSET—I EMBRACE MY FEAR

We all face fear. Regardless of how hard you may try and how much planning you do, you'll never remove it completely from your life. But the fear is part of what makes you stronger. If you didn't have fear, there wouldn't be anything for you to overcome. See, courage isn't about not being scared. It's about being scared and doing it anyway.

The ability to act in spite of fear is a big part of what makes you a man. Fear is not a barrier to what you want most; it's an indicator that you're about to be pushed outside your comfort zone. Being pushed outside your comfort zone could potentially pose a very real and serious threat to your well-being, or it could simply mean you're about to be tested, which, in turn, will make you stronger. In other words, fear is our brain's way of telling us we're about to do something incredibly brave or something incredibly stupid. I think we all inherently know what that line is.

If fear is no longer viewed as a real and tangible factor but rather something to be listened to and understood, we should not shun fear but embrace it. We should thank the fear for telling us what we need to know and for guiding us to something we should engage in. Frankly put, we should embrace it. It's there to help.

This is one of the reasons my favorite superhero is Batman. He could have let his fear of bats cripple him and keep him from doing what his heart was calling him to do. But he didn't. He decided instead to embrace the thing he feared most and harness its power to produce an effective outcome. But the bat is just an analogy. It's an analogy for your own primal fears. What is it that you fear most? Rejection? Failure? Ridicule?

If that's the case and you choose to run and hide, you will always be exposed by the fear you're hiding from. You will always feel inadequate. You will always play it safe. You will always attempt to fit in by changing who you are and who you're meant to be.

The only way to overcome the feeling of fear is to recognize it and drive forward anyway. I was scared to start playing football until I started playing football. I was scared of basic training until I went to basic training. I was scared to marry my wife until I married my wife. I was scared to become a father until I became a father. I was scared to start a business until I started a business.

This isn't permission to be reckless. It's permission to do the things you know you should. The further you run from fear, the more vulnerable you become. When you turn around, embrace the fear, and take action, you take back the power you've been giving away for so long.

THE SKILL SET

Foster Courage. Fortunately, courage is something that can be developed and fostered in your life. You can't expect to go from a timid, captive man to one who owns all his fears overnight. It doesn't work like that.

Like any muscle that needs to be developed, you'll need to develop the muscle of courage. Developing this muscle is as simple as starting out small. If, for example, you're deathly afraid of public speaking (like I was for a long time), you don't need to go present to an audience of two thousand, two hundred, or even twenty, initially. The first step may be to speak to the mirror, followed by speaking in front of a camera, followed by speaking in front of family, followed by friends, and so on.

Just be careful not to get comfortable with doing less than you know you should be doing. If, after showing courage toward something, you no longer feel the fear, it means it's time to step up your game.

Practicing courage makes it easier to display courage when it's required. Archilochus said, "We don't rise to the level of our expectations, we fall to the level of our training." So when you sense fear welling up inside you, act on it. Make a statement in a board meeting you normally wouldn't make. Sign up for a 5k, knowing that you want to run a marathon one day. Strike up a conversation with a woman at work before asking the girl in your class on a date. There are thousands of ways to display courage without placing yourself in any real danger. The more you do it, the better at it you become.

Contingencies. I know it's popular to believe that you should burn the boats. In many cases you should. But not in every case.

Especially when you're making moves that expose you and/or your family to potential loss.

It sounds really good: "Burn the boats." "Go all in." "No plan B." But no war general would go into battle without identifying potential threats to his strategy and implementing tactics to ensure minimal loss to the cause.

The same holds true for the decisions you make in your life. You don't need to quit your job on a whim with no savings just to prove you're courageous. You don't need to go run a marathon without the proper training just so you can overcome fear. You don't need to launch a business without doing some research to test a viable business strategy.

Contingencies, in many cases, are the strategies and plans that allow you to take action. When I launched Order of Man, it was much easier for me to make it work because I had steady, reliable income from my financial planning practice. Some might say I was less courageous than the guy who launched his business with no money and no backup plan. That might be true. Then again, I might just have been smarter.

Identify the gaps in your actions. Look for possible threats and weaknesses to your well-being. Develop contingencies to address them. Be calculated. Be smart. Then, be courageous.

PART IV

THE BATTLE

PLAN

"Life brings sorrows and joys alike. It's what a man does with them—not what they do to him—that is the true test of his mettle."
-Theodore Roosevelt

We have talked about so much up to this point. We've talked about the Battle being waged against us by outside sources and by ourselves. We've talked about our mission as men: protect, provide, preside. And we've talked about the Code of Conduct by which the Sovereign Man operates his life.

The battle is what we're up against. The mission is our ultimate purpose and gives us a sense of purpose and direction. And the Code of Conduct represents the manner in which we pursue the mission.

Now, we're going to talk about the way we actually make this work. Up until this point, most of what we've addressed has been the thirty thousand–foot view. It's been the back story. It's been the philosophical side of the Sovereign Man. All of these are critical to recapturing your sovereignty, but they don't paint the entire picture.

What good is it to know if we can't do? I have a friend who entered the financial planning industry at the same time as I did. As we were learning the ropes of the industry and bouncing ideas off each other, he would often ask, "Therefore what?" as I would talk about what was wrong with the industry and how we should be able to be much more productive than we were. What he was asking is what we should do with the information I was sharing. In other words, he was asking, "Now what?"

In Part IV, we uncover a very specific strategy I've discovered, developed, modified, tweaked, and adjusted over the course of the last eight years, which has allowed me to produce big results in the relationship I have with my wife and children; my mental, emotional, and physical health; my two businesses; and my finances.

This is the Battle Plan. It's a very tactical process that answers the question, "Now what?"

See, most men inherently know to some extent what they should be doing with their lives. They have a loose idea of what they want, and they can certainly feel that something's missing. This missing piece is how to actually go about reclaiming their sovereign power.

In the chapters that follow, we uncover a five-step, action-driven process designed to take control of your life. First, we cover the importance of articulating a vision that will pull you toward and through the actions needed to achieve sovereignty. We also talk about identifying objectives you feel are important on your own personal journey in four key areas of your life (the Four Quadrants). Next, we walk you through the process of "reverse engineering" the entire plan in order to uncover the key tactics you'll use to reach your objectives. From there, we'll help you establish checkpoints to ensure you're on the right path. Lastly, we wrap up with the concept of the After-Action Review to ensure you're meeting your objectives and setting new ones effectively.

A battle cannot be won without a plan. If by some miracle it is, it's not replicable. In the pages that follow, you're going to learn a system that will allow you to produce results over and over and over again.

None of what you've read up until now will matter if you cannot make a plan and work the plan. I'll show you how to do both.

CHAPTER 20

VISION

"Here is the manliness of manhood, that a man has a good reason for what he does, and has a will in doing it."
-Alexander MacLaren

Without a clear vision for what you want out of life, you have no hope of accomplishing anything meaningful. Sure, you may stumble onto some success here and there, but if you don't know where you're going, you'll have no benchmark by which to measure your behaviors and actions, and the success you may have enjoyed will dwindle away as quickly as you may have acquired it.

Most men lack vision. They so consume themselves with the day-to-day operations of their lives that they forget to take (or simply don't have) the time to ponder what a well-lived life actually looks like. It's a lot like running with your head down, only to look up and realize you've been running in the wrong direction for far too long.

One of the most common questions I'm asked is whether a man should take a job that would offer more pay but keep him away from his family, or settle for less pay but be physically and mentally present and available to his wife and children. That's a question I can't answer for another man, but what I suggest is that the man who is debating this choice project himself twenty to thirty years into the future. Which decision will he be glad he made? With that, typically he comes to his own conclusion regarding what he should do. This is the power of having clearly articulated vision.

The first step in creating a Battle Plan that will allow you to recapture your sovereignty is to spend some serious time thinking about what you want your life to look like—one actually worth fighting for. I realize this can be a tall order, considering that a lot of men haven't given the future too much thought. More often than not, all they know is they aren't happy with their current life.

To that, I have to ask, what's the alternative? If you're in a dead-end job, what would a better job look like? If you're in a struggling marriage, how would a successful marriage feel? If your health is deteriorating, what would life be like if you were strong and energized?

These are the types of questions you have to start asking yourself. See, I think a lot of men are hoping they can read this book or sign up for that program or listen to a podcast and get the answers they're looking for. It doesn't work like that. You aren't entitled to the answers you're after. You have to earn them.

I wish I could tell you what your future should look like, but if I did, it would have no relevancy or significance to you. A vision for the future is deeply personal and very individualized. And it requires a lot of thought and a lot of effort.

Now, before I get to some exercises that I'm going to ask you to complete, I need to tell you that there is no right or wrong way to do this. Too many men won't get started with these exercises or will give up too quickly because they think they're doing it wrong or they're not good enough at it. That belief does not serve you. The belief that you're learning a new operating system and it will take time to develop does.

As Theodore Roosevelt would say, "Do what you can, with what you have, where you are." Be patient. Be honest. Trust the process.

EXERCISES

Below, I'm going to walk you through a series of four exercises to help you begin to develop a clear vision for yourself.

First, I'm going to share some insights on visions that pull (positive reinforcement) you toward something worthwhile. Next, we'll begin to uncover visions that push (negative reinforcement) you toward a new reality. Third, we'll begin to articulate the new man you'll need to become in order to fulfill the vision you have for yourself. And last, you'll be asked to write your own eulogy as an exercise in looking at things from a new perspective.

These exercises are done at your discretion. No one is going to be here to hold your hand or make you accountable. You have the ultimate say in how much attention and effort you give them. I encourage you to be as thorough as possible. It's easy to skim the surface and settle for "good enough," but that's not the way of the Sovereign Man. These exercises highlight the foundation principle of an effective Battle Plan: make it count.

THE PULL

Take an inventory in your life and think about the times you've been the most satisfied, the most content, and the most fulfilled. These are the things that are going to pull you to become the man you have a desire to become.

For me, I think about my four children and my beautiful wife. I think about what a deep and meaningful relationship with them would look like. I envision sitting on the porch with them, having conversations about life. I can feel the laughter as we sit around the dinner table, joking about our daily activities.

When I think about my work, I think about the millions of men who would benefit from the work I'm doing. I can see the e-mails and messages I receive every day from those men who have been positively impacted by the mission we're on. I can feel a sense of pride and satisfaction as I experience and become part of their personal victories.

When I think about my health, I envision being strong, lean, and capable of handling anything that life may have to throw at me. I can see myself fitting into my shirt a bit better and the compliments I receive from my wife when she says she likes the way a pair of jeans fits on me. I see my children and me bouncing on the trampoline and running around outside for hours.

I also think about my community. I see the young men in our neighborhood learning life lessons from the football, basketball, and baseball teams I coach. I see a neighbor in need and me having the capacity to serve them. I see myself at some future date serving in charitable organizations and giving freely of my time and money.

These visions are a powerfully emotional experience and give me a deep desire to be a Sovereign Man—a protector, provider, and presider.

What do you see when you look at your relationships, your business, your community, your health, and your life?

_____

_____

_____

_____

_____

_____

_____

_____

_____

_____

_____

_____

_____

THE PUSH

Now, take an inventory of your life and consider all the negative experiences that drive you to become a better man. These are the things that are going to drive you to do something different in your life so you can produce a different outcome.

For me, I think about what it was like to grow up without a permanent father figure in my life. I can vividly remember how I felt when I would see other kids go on campouts with their father and the frustration I experienced when I didn't have that for myself.

I can remember my wife leaving with my six-month-old son and wondering how in the world I was ever going to get them back. I remember the dark and lonely nights and the bitterness, anger, and resentment I felt.

I look back to the days when I was fifty pounds heavier than I am today. I remember not being able to play with my kids and not being physically attractive for my wife. I remember finding out she didn't enjoy having sex with me because the physical attraction wasn't there for her. I remember being exhausted at the end of the day and not being able to do anything except plop my fat ass on the couch. There was a sense of helplessness I never wanted to experience again.

For all these reasons and so many more, I wanted to grow and expand and become a new man. I'm still on this journey.

What do you see and remember that you do not wish to experience again in your life? What feelings do you wish to avoid and will do anything you can to keep yourself from experiencing?

_____

_____

_____

_____

_____

_____

WHAT KIND OF MAN?

In order to achieve the pulling and avoid the pushing vision you've identified, you are going to need to become a new man. It's been said that if you want something you have never had, you must be willing do something you have never done. I would also add that you're going to need to be something you've never been.

When I think about the man I need to become in order to realize the vision I have for myself, I can see that I'll need to be strong, courageous, bold, compassionate, kind, caring, and honorable. I can see that I'll need to be diligent in my pursuit of mastery. I can see that I'll need to be patient with my wife and children. I can see that I'll also need to be patient with the results in my business. I'll need to learn to be a more effective communicator and a powerful networker. I'll need to find ways to add value to other people. I'll need to develop the confidence to ask people to do business with me and support me in my ventures. And I'll need to take massive action toward the results I desire.

What kind of man will you need to be as you begin to articulate the vision you have for yourself and your life?

_____

_____

_____

_____

_____

_____

_____

_____

_____

_____

_____

_____

_____

WRITE YOUR OWN EULOGY

At first glance, the notion of writing your own eulogy may appear to be a morbid exercise. I agree, it is. But I encourage you to look deeper than that and recognize the power it has to give you a new perspective on the life you're working to create. When we give ourselves the opportunity to look at our experiences from a different point of view, we often uncover new ideas, thoughts, and insights into how we wish to live our life.

As you write your eulogy, keep in mind this is not an exercise in the way people would remember you for the way you currently are, but for the way you wish to become.

Where did you live? What education do you have? What does your family look like? When others describe you, what will they say? How did you die? How did you live? What did you do for fun? Who were your friends? How did you show up? How did people feel when they were around you? What will others miss about you? The more of these deep questions you can answer, the better.

As I considered sharing this exercise, I thought initially I should include my own eulogy. But the more I considered it, the more I thought I should withhold it. Remember, there is no right or wrong way to do this. Letting you operate from a blank slate gives you the freedom to really think and explore what you would want your life to look like. Take some time and really be thorough in what you write.

_____

_____

_____

_____

_____

_____

_____

_____

_____

_____

_____

_____

_____

_____

_____

_____

_____

_____

_____

_____

_____

_____

_____

_____

_____

_____

_____

As you work through these exercises, keep in mind that they are likely to take longer than a single sitting. Creating a compelling vision is a work in progress and, regardless of how far along the path you are, you should always be visiting your vision and working through the exercises. Please also remember that going through this work is not an opportunity to beat yourself up for doing it incorrectly. There is no right or wrong way. This is merely the beginning of a lifelong pursuit of sovereignty. You will become a master, but for right now, I'm just asking you to start.

CHAPTER 21

OBJECTIVES

"If a man knows not to which port he sails, no wind is favorable."
-Seneca

At this point, you have begun to work on your vision for the future. You've thought about what you want your life to look like with regard to your relationships, your business, your health, and every other facet of your life. You've tapped into the power of projecting yourself into the future and looking back on your life to determine what it is that you actually want and how it feels to have it.

As powerful an exercise as visualization can be, it does nothing to move the needle. Sure, it's a great place to start, but until you begin to identify what specifically you're after, your vision will remain a dream—nothing less, nothing more.

The second step in the Battle Plan is to articulate your objective. What is it that you're actually after? How will you determine if you're winning the battle for your sovereignty?

One of the most challenging times in my life was my deployment in Iraq. I did believe we were engaging in a noble calling. I saw the victories we had with the civilians we dealt with. I saw Iraqi men overcoming fear, threats, and potential violence to volunteer for the Iraqi police force. With so much good that came from our operations, it was hard to see the men and women I served with give so much of themselves without a clear objective. At times, it felt as if we were spinning our wheels without getting anywhere. Quite honestly, it's hard to win a battle in which a victory or failure has not been defined.

So it is with your life. Go ask ten people how they're doing today, and you're likely to be met with, "I'm doing great. Extremely busy." It's as if somehow being busy is the benchmark of victory. I don't know about you, but I don't want to be busy. I want to be effective. I want to be efficient. I want to be pursuing an actual objective.

It's easy for a man to do a bunch of work, but if that work isn't getting the job done, does the work even matter? Developing and identifying an objective is the benchmark by which you judge your work. Remember, the goal isn't to be busy. It's to be effective. (We'll talk more about this in Chapter 22.)

In order to be effective, you have to know what you're working toward. You have to have an objective.

THE FOUR QUADRANTS

Before we move ahead, it's important that we narrow this down even further. A lot of times, when I talk with men about developing and identifying objectives, they want to change every single thing about their lives. While I can appreciate the desire and initiative, it isn't feasible to change it all—at least not right away. Some of that change will take years, and other changes will simply be a by-product of focusing on four key areas, or quadrants, of your life. The Four Quadrants are Calibration, Connection, Condition, and Contribution.

It's so easy to get overwhelmed. It's likely that, since you're this far in the book, you have a huge desire to get started and reclaim your sovereignty. Good. That's what I want for you. But if you can't sustain the activity, it's not going to do you any good.

Besides, if you spread your attention too thin, you become ineffective at it all. I want you to focus on four key areas. And, even deeper, one element in each of the quadrants I'll be sharing with you. When you give your utmost attention to these quadrants, everything else in your life will seem to align. These quadrants represent the low-hanging fruit and have the greatest potential to permeate every aspect of your life.

Calibration. Calibration is about getting right with yourself first. Too many men focus on others first because they believe that is what is required of a man. Unfortunately, they focus too heavily on others at the expense of their own well-being. If you truly want to help others on your journey, you have to ensure you're capable of doing so, which means taking care of yourself. Calibration represents your mental and emotional health, mindset, psyche, soul, and spirituality.

Connection. Connection is the focus of building deep and powerful relationships with your family, colleagues, neighbors, coworkers, and band of brothers. There is no such thing as a self-made man. Every man must learn to connect with others across all facets of life to ensure he and others are successful.

Condition. Condition is the focus on your physical health—more specifically, diet, nutrition, fitness, exercise, sleep, stamina, strength, and conditioning. It is impossible to become the man you are meant to be without the ability to keep your body in optimal working order.

Contribution. Contribution is your ability to become a man of value. At times, you will be compensated for your contribution (employment, for example). Other times, you will not (service and charitable work). Whether you're trying to connect with your family and friends, launch a business, and/or grow your bank account, your ability to contribute more than you currently do will make all the difference.

As we move into the recommended time frame for your objectives, I want you to think about the one thing you want to focus on in each of these quadrants that will help make your vision a reality. I know there's a lot you want to do, but you'll have time to get to all of it. Right now, start thinking about the one thing that will make the absolute biggest difference.

THE NEXT TWELVE WEEKS

Now that you have an idea of where you'll be focusing your attention, let's talk about the time frame for your objectives. There has been a lot of talk on the length of objectives. Should you have short-term objectives (less than twelve months) or long-term objectives (longer than twelve months)?

Personally, I opt to go with Twelve-Week Objectives. Now, some people will tell me I should have long-term objectives for myself. Some even suggest I should plan things out for five years. I don't even know what I'm going to have for dinner tonight, let alone what I'm going to be doing in five years and what resources will be available to me at that time. Don't get me wrong, having a sense of direction for long periods of time is powerful, but anything longer than twelve weeks should fall under the category of vision, not objectives.

Twelve-Week Objectives have served me best because they're long enough to make a meaningful and measurable difference in my life, and they're short enough to keep my attention and focus.

If you make your objectives too long, you run the risk of burning yourself out before you produce the results you're after in your life. If you make your objectives too short, you'll likely produce less than you're capable of producing because you don't have adequate time to produce significant results.

Another benefit of Twelve-Week Objectives is that you'll have an added level of flexibility in your Battle Plan. Life happens. We get sidetracked. We get sued. We get hurt. Plans change, as do priorities. The last thing you want to do is lock yourself into a plan that relies on your working at it for the next five years with no room to maneuver and shift should there be changes to your life internally or externally.

The purpose of Twelve-Week Objectives is to create laser-like focus in your planning. Everyone can be focused for twelve weeks. That's ninety days of undivided attention toward your objectives in each of the Four Quadrants.

SPECIFICITY

Before I give you the questions to ask yourself and the time to identify your own Twelve-Week Objectives in each of the Four Quadrants, I need you to understand that the more specific you can get in your objectives, the more likely you will be to experience results.

It's not enough to say, "I want to be healthy." Welcome to the club. Everyone wants that. What exactly does that look like for you? Is it being twenty pounds lighter? Is it having 10 percent body fat? Is it the ability to run a certain distance without stopping? Is it the ability to deadlift a certain amount? What exactly are you after?

I've often found that if it can be objectively measured, you're on the right track. If you say, "I want to be rich," that's relative. The answer is different for everyone. But if you say, "I want to be making twenty thousand dollars per month in the next ninety days," that can be objectively measured. There's no guesswork as to what that means.

Let me give you some alternatives to common (and overly general) objectives.

"I want to do more things for myself" should be measured by time engaged in an activity, proficiency at a certain skill, development of a specific hobby, time alone, books read, etc.

"I want to have a great connection with my wife" should be measured by conversations had, dates had, frequency of sex, arguments neutralized, vacations attended, etc.

"I want to be healthy" should be measured by body weight, body fat percentage, weight lifted, distance run, time run, hours of sleep per night, daily caloric intake, daily caloric deficit, etc.

"I want to be better off financially" should be measured by income, expenses, debt ratio, savings and investments, assets, liabilities, etc.

As we get into the questions and your own twelve-week objectives, get hyper-specific. Don't worry that you're not focused on all you want to accomplish right now. You'll have time to get to new objectives in twelve weeks.

TWELVE-WEEK OBJECTIVES

Now, let's move on to identifying your Twelve-Week Objectives in each of the Four Quadrants. As you identify your objectives, I would urge you to be assertive. Instead of using soft language like "I'd like to," "I hope to," "Maybe I will," "If I can," and "I'll try my best," use assertive statements like "I will." For example, "I will lose twenty pounds in the next ninety days."

Let's get started.

What is your Twelve-Week Objective for Calibration?

Examples: I will read five books in the next ninety days.
I will shave three strokes off my golf game in the next ninety days.
I will finish the woodworking project I started in the next ninety days.

I will rebuild the engine I've been working on in the next ninety days.

I will meditate for twenty hours total in the next ninety days.

_____

_____

_____

_____

What is your Twelve-Week Objective for Connection?

Examples: I will plan and finalize our family vacation in the next ninety days.

I will give my wife fifty hours of undivided attention in the next ninety days.

I will coach my son's basketball team over the next ninety days.

I will hold performance reviews with all of my employees in the next ninety days.

I will plan and finalize a hunt with my friends in the next ninety days.

_____

_____

_____

_____

What is your Twelve-Week Objective for Condition?

Examples: I will run a Spartan Race in the next ninety days

I will perform a four-hundred-pound deadlift next ninety days.

I will lose twenty pounds in the next nin

I will reach 15 percent body fat in the next ninety days.

I will run a marathon in the next ninety days.

_____

_____

_____

_____

What is your Twelve-Week Objective for Contribution?

Examples: I will complete my book in the next ninety days.

I will secure a promotion in the next ninety days.

I will increase my income to ten thousand dollars per month in the next ninety days.

I will launch my new business in the next ninety days.

I will serve on a charitable board in the next ninety days.

_____

_____

_____

_____

Armed with your Twelve-Week Objectives, you now have a goal for each of the Four Quadrants. This doesn't necessarily make things easier, but it does give you the power that comes only from having direction in your life.

Please understand, before we get into the tactics, things are going to come up that may keep you from accomplishing your objectives. If you do get derailed, do not get discouraged. Simply wipe yourself off, recommit to your objectives (tweak them as needed), and re-engage in the battle.

Answering the questions below in each of the Four Quadrants will also help keep you from getting distracted and failing in the completion of your objectives.

Why are these Twelve-Week Objectives important to me?

_____

_____

_____

What will it look and feel like when I accomplish these objectives?

_____

_____

_____

What is the cost of not achieving these objectives?

_____

_____

_____

What situations could arise that would keep me from accomplishing what I set out to do?

_____

_____

_____

How will I handle these situations when they arise?

_____

_____

_____

How will I celebrate the completion of my Twelve-Week Objectives?

_____

_____

_____

CHAPTER 22

TACTICS

"Let us remember that, as much has been given us, much will be expected from us; and that true homage comes from the heart as well as from the lips and shows itself in deeds."
-Theodore Roosevelt

We've all heard the adage to "begin with the end in mind." The key word is "begin," which suggests there's more to it than simply articulating a vision and a few objectives for your life. Unfortunately, too many men focus solely on their ultimate objective and never give any real consideration to how they're actually going to accomplish it.

Great, you want to lose weight or start a business or make money or connect with your wife. How are you going to do it? Usually when I ask this question I get the deer-in-the-headlights stare. It's as if these men believe that just because they've dedicated a very limited amount of time and energy to thinking about what they want, they're miraculously entitled to the reality of their desires. Do you honestly believe it's just going to happen? Do you really think that the world is going to bow down to you and your every wish simply because you hope it will?

The answer is obviously no. I think it's safe to assume we'd all answer that way, but when it really comes down to it, there are way too many men whose actions (or lack thereof) would prove otherwise.

Up to this point, we've done a lot of reflection about what you'd like your future to look like and what exactly you want to accomplish, but that's the easy part. What I'm asking you to do now is to identify the action required to produce the desired objectives.

What can you do on a daily basis that will naturally and inevitably produce the result you're after? This is where your time and energy should be spent—not daydreaming about what could be but actively making it happen.

See, the process of articulating your vision and identifying your objectives is simply a means to an end—a starting point for developing an actual strategy to recapture your sovereignty.

REVERSE ENGINEERING

The first thing you need to wrap your head around is the idea that you are reverse engineering a plan that will accomplish the desired objective. Think about the last time you took a road trip. You started with where you were, you looked where you were going, then you researched the routes available to get from point A to point B. After that, it was a matter of picking the best route and starting to drive.

The same holds true for identifying tactics. Very simply, your tactics are the route that will get you to where you're going most effectively.

Now, to stick with our analogy, let's say that you have three days to get to your final destination. Once you know that, you can work backward into markers along the journey that you need to hit by a certain time—checkpoints.

Armed with these checkpoints and tactics, you can now execute the plan and measure your progress along the way. This is a very simple process. Many men will overlook it because it is so simple.

But nowhere does it say that your planning has to be a challenge for it to be effective. Occam's razor states that the simpler option is typically the better option. Do not overthink this process. If you do, you'll stall out and abandon the system that has the power to transform your life.

CHECKPOINTS

Let's cover checkpoints first. I'm not going to go into too much detail on this because it's pretty self-explanatory. Knowing that you now have a ninety-day objective in each of the Four Quadrants, you are going to create two checkpoints along the way—one at thirty days and one at sixty days.

This is an often-overlooked part of the planning process. The reason it's crucial that you come up with two checkpoints is twofold.

First, having two checkpoints along the way will help you maintain motivation on your journey. These checkpoints will allow you to see your progress and that your actions are truly producing results. It's easy to get discouraged if you can't see or don't track the tangible results of your efforts. If in thirty days you see progress, you're likely to continue the course of action. If you have to wait until ninety days, you may not.

The second reason you'll want to identify checkpoints is to "adjust fire" along the way should you need to. Look, it's possible that your plan isn't working. If that's the case, we don't want to wait until the twelve weeks are up to come to that realization. You want to find out quickly and make the required adjustments to ensure you hit your objective on time and on target.

In the questions below, you'll find room to identify both your thirty- and sixty-day checkpoints along with examples based on sample Twelve-Week Objectives.

Sample Calibration Objective: I will read six books in the next ninety days.

Thirty-Day Checkpoint Example: I will have completed two books.
Sixty-Day Checkpoint Example: I will have completed four books.

What is the Twelve-Week Calibration Objective you identified from the previous chapter?_____

_____

_____

_____

What are your thirty and sixty-day checkpoints?

Thirty-Day Checkpoint: _____
Sixty-Day Checkpoint: _____

Sample Connection Objective: I will plan/finalize our family vacation in the next ninety days.

Thirty-Day Checkpoint Example: I will have completed the logistics and planning.
Sixty-Day Checkpoint Example: I will have fully funded the vacation.

What is the Twelve-Week Connection Objective you identified from the previous chapter?_____

_____

_____

_____

What are your thirty- and sixty-day checkpoints?

Thirty-Day Checkpoint: _____

Sixty-Day Checkpoint: _____

Sample Condition Objective: I will perform a 400-pound deadlift in ninety days.

Thirty-Day Checkpoint Example: I will have completed a 360-pound deadlift.
Sixty-Day Checkpoint Example: I will have completed a 380-pound deadlift.

What is the Twelve-Week Condition Objective you identified from the previous chapter?_____

_____

_____

_____

What are your thirty- and sixty-day checkpoints?

Thirty-Day Checkpoint: _____

Sixty-Day Checkpoint: _____

Sample Contribution Objective: I will launch my business in the next ninety days.

Thirty-Day Checkpoint Example: I will have finalized the branding (images, logos, naming, etc.).
Sixty-Day Checkpoint Example: I will have completed the website and social media platforms.

What is the Twelve-Week Contribution Objective you identified from the previous chapter?_____

_____

_____

_____

What are your thirty- and sixty-day checkpoints?

Thirty-Day Checkpoint: _____

Sixty-Day Checkpoint: _____

PRIMARY AND SECONDARY TACTICS ─────────────────────

Now that you've identified your checkpoints, it's time to come up with two tactics in each of the Four Quadrants that will ensure you hit both your checkpoints and your final objective. When coming up with the tactics you will focus on, strive to find something you can complete every single day.

A huge factor in determining the success of your objectives is your ability to be consistent. If you choose tactics that are completed every two weeks, for example, there is no consistency in that, and you will have a difficult time developing the habit of action required to succeed over and over and over again.

Also, you'll notice I said "two tactics." Not three. Not seven. Only two. If you spread yourself too thin on the actions you'll be taking, you're likely to burn out. Focusing on just two tactics also forces you to choose actions that will yield the biggest results. Remember, we're about efficiency, not busywork.

To go even further, when determining which tactics to implement, you will be asked to identify a primary tactic (completed every day) and a secondary tactic (a onetime or once-per-week tactic). Focus on your primary tactic. Only give attention to the secondary tactic as needed, if at all (some objectives do not require a secondary tactic).

Remember, as you identify tactics, you are not locking yourself into these actions forever. You're only planning for the next twelve weeks, which means you'll be doing this four times per year. You may also be required to change tactics midway through your Battle Plan because, during the review of your checkpoints, you might realize the tactics you're currently employing are not producing the desired results.

This is merely planning. It may be appropriate and even necessary to change strategies once you're engaged in the fight. Understand that now and be willing to be flexible in order to achieve the results you are fighting for.

Sample Calibration Objective: I will read six books in the next ninety days.

Primary Tactic: Read for thirty minutes every day.
Secondary Tactic: Read for two hours every weekend.

What are your Primary and Secondary Tactics for your Calibration Objective?

Primary Tactic (to be completed daily): _____

_____

Secondary Tactic (to be completed periodically, if at all): _____

_____

Sample Connection Objective: I will plan/finalize our family vacation in the next ninety days.

Primary Tactic: Save twenty-five dollars per day.
Secondary Tactic: Research activities and locations every weekend.

What are your Primary and Secondary Tactics for your Connection Objective?

Primary Tactic (to be completed daily): _____

_____

Secondary Tactic (to be completed periodically, if at all): _____

_____

Sample Condition Objective: I will perform a 400-pound deadlift in ninety days.

Primary Tactic: Exercise for sixty minutes per day.
Secondary Tactic: Test for maximum deadlift every two weeks.

What are your Primary and Secondary Tactics for your Condition Objective?

Primary Tactic (to be completed daily): _____

_____

Secondary Tactic (to be completed periodically, if at all): _____

_____

Sample Contribution Objective: I will launch my business in the next ninety days.

Primary Tactic: Spend sixty minutes per day developing the business.
Secondary Tactic: Spend an hour per week with a business mentor.

What are your Primary and Secondary Tactics for your Contribution Objective?

Primary Tactic (to be completed daily): _____

_____

Secondary Tactic (to be completed periodically, if at all): _____

_____

CHAPTER 23

AFTER-ACTION REVIEW

"Look not mournfully into the past. It comes not back again. Wisely improve the present. It is thine. Go forth to meet the shadowy future, without fear, and a manly heart."

-Henry Wadsworth Longfellow

If there's one thing that has the power to continue your growth and expansion, and maintain your sovereignty long after the motivation of this book wears off, it's an After-Action Review.

See, most men go about their duties, they do some planning here and there, they keep their head down, and they hope it all works out. Hope, however, is not a strategy. When we overlook the power of reviewing our work, we subject ourselves to the mercy of external sources. Hopefully the market will work out. Hopefully the president will make wise decisions. Hopefully my boss likes my work. Hopefully I never get sick. Hopefully, hopefully, hopefully.

I don't know about you, but I'd rather place my future in something a bit more tangible and predictable. Not that everything is always going to work out when you make a plan, execute the plan, and review it. Things don't always work out the way we hope they will, but whether victorious or disastrous, there is always something to be learned and improved upon.

This is where the After-Action Review comes into play. Essentially, the After-Action Review is a series of five questions that you should ask yourself after every engagement, encounter, exercise, project, conversation, and/or activity. Armed with the answers to these five questions, you will give yourself exponential opportunity to learn from your experiences and master whatever you happen to engage in.

If you've spent any time in the military or law enforcement, you're probably somewhat familiar with the After-Action Review. I was introduced to it when I joined the National Guard, and, at the time, I hated it. Honestly, it seemed like just another task we had to check off without any real purpose or effect on our ability to improve performance. That may have been because it was handled ineffectively or because, in my youth, I allowed my arrogance and ego to get in the way. After all, if I had to consider what I might improve, what did that say about my initial performance in the first place?

But this isn't an opportunity to talk about all the things you did wrong. The After-Action Review is also an opportunity to uncover your strengths and what you did right. This is an opportunity to take an objective look at your performance and double down on your strengths and shore up any weaknesses.

This one strategy has illuminated all kinds of gaps in my actions and highlighted things that would have been difficult for me to discover without it. When I first learned the After-Action Review, I had to reference the questions, but I've used it so often now (dozens of times per day), that I've internalized the questions and can quickly break down what I did right and where I went wrong in any activity.

Yes, I want you to use the answers to the After-Action Review Questions to review your Twelve-Week Battle Plan, but I also want you to use them after difficult conversations, projects at work, hobbies you're attempting to master, and the way you complete your tasks around the house.

The more you use these questions, the more powerful you become in expanding your skill set and sovereignty.

WHAT DID I ACCOMPLISH?

The first question in the After-Action Review is "What did I accomplish?" At the end of the day, did you accomplish what you set out to accomplish? In order to have a level of measurable success, you have to identify objectives in the first place. If you don't, how will you ever know if you're producing desired results? You won't.

Take a look at your Battle Plan and, specifically, your objectives in each of the Four Quadrants. Did you accomplish your objective? Be truthful with yourself. You either did or you didn't. You might be able to fool others with the answer to this question, but you cannot fool yourself.

If you can answer yes to this question, congratulations. Now go back to the drawing board and create a new objective that will push you further than your recent victory.

If the answer is no, you have some work to do. But take heart. In answering this and the remaining questions, you are arming yourself with an opportunity to get it right next time around.

WHAT DID I NOT ACCOMPLISH?

It's safe to assume that whether or not you completed your objective, there were probably some metrics in which you fell short and have some room for improvement in. Perhaps you completed your objective early but failed to recalibrate and push yourself as hard as you know you could have. Maybe you completed a portion of your objective but missed other parts of it. Maybe you didn't accomplish anything at all.

Whatever the outcome, accepting the reality that there were some areas in which you missed the mark is critical if you are to maximize your potential and outcomes moving forward.

The answer to this question may also represent your objective for the next twelve weeks. Remember, missing an objective is not the end of the world. We're in this thing for the long haul.

When answering this question, it's also important to ask yourself why you fell short. Was the goal too ambitious? Were there some things that came up that you need to plan for next time? What was the reason for your failure? (Note, I said "reason," not "excuse.")

WHAT DID I DO WELL?

Each and every one of us has a certain set of strengths. Far too often men fail to recognize what these actually are. If you knew for certain what you were good at and where you were most effective, you could craft a plan around those strengths to produce exponential results.

So, whether you completed your objective or not, this is an opportunity for you to start uncovering the strengths you bring to the table. Were you extremely organized? Were you consistent with your tactics? Did you do a good job communicating your vision and plan to those who would be impacted by the decisions you were making? When you got off track, were you able to adjust and make corrections quickly? Were there elements of your Battle Plan that seemed to come easy for you?

These are all powerful questions that will begin to highlight where you are naturally inclined to succeed. I can't tell you how often I've heard my children complain that life isn't fair. We, as parents, typically brush it off as best we can, but our kids are right—life isn't fair. There are some skill sets, traits, and talents that you possess that push the odds in your favor. Your goal should be to uncover what they are and use them to your benefit.

WHAT DID I NOT DO WELL?

Just as you possess a set of strengths, you also possess a set of weaknesses. It's a fact, you can't be good at everything. So, on your journey to complete your Twelve-Week Battle Plan, you likely recognized some areas where you really struggled.

Did you have a hard time tracking your activity? Were you able to maintain consistency? Did you notice yourself getting distracted from your tactics? Did you have a tendency to rationalize your inaction? Did you burn out quickly? Did you let others deter you from driving on?

The answers to these questions will help you see where you may need to develop a new set of skills and potentially bring in someone or something else to help you achieve more. Is there work that can be delegated, for example? Or technology that will tighten up some of the areas in which you struggle?

I personally struggle with the details. They're boring, tiresome, and draining. But I also recognize the need for details. So, rather than trouble myself with getting caught up in the specifics, I've hired someone who is very detail oriented and thrives on the specific planning I hate. This way, the needs and objectives are met, and I can focus on the things I excel in.

WHAT WILL I DO DIFFERENTLY MOVING FORWARD?

This is the most powerful question in the After-Action Review and one you must answer if you want to improve moving forward. It's easy to do something for twelve weeks, then completely forget about it and neglect to maintain the changes you've made in your life.

We're after lasting changes here, not temporary ones. So, after every Twelve-Week Battle Plan, you should ask yourself what you are going to do differently next time. Or how you are going to expand on the actions you've taken up to this point.

We've talked about life being a process of experimentation. That's exactly what this question alludes to. Through the process of the Battle Plan and, specifically, the After-Action Review, you're setting yourself up for the next twelve-week experimentation.

You're going to find that some of your experiments work and others do not. Your mission is to identify and keep what works and strip away anything that does not.

When answering this question, you will want to look to behaviors, resources, people, technology, information, and/or ideas you need to incorporate to make things more effective next time around.

Maybe you've identified your need to bring in a new teammate on a project. Maybe you need to double down your efforts in certain areas. Maybe you need to research more before engaging in an activity. Maybe your level of preparation was off, and you need to do more of that moving forward. Or maybe what you did actually worked perfectly, and it's something you're going to adopt permanently into the way you live your life.

Whatever you uncover though the five questions comprising the After-Action Review, always transition into the next project, idea, conversation, activity, and/or Battle Plan with clear answers to these questions and a plan to get better moving forward.

THE AFTER-ACTION REVIEW

What did I accomplish?

_____

_____

_____

_____

_____

_____

_____

_____

_____

_____

_____

What did I not accomplish?

_____

_____

_____

_____

_____

_____

_____

_____

_____

_____

_____

_____

_____

_____

What did I do well?

_____

_____

_____

_____

_____

_____

_____

_____

_____

_____

_____

_____

_____

_____

What did I not do well?

_____
_____
_____
_____
_____
_____
_____
_____
_____
_____
_____
_____
_____

What will I do differently moving forward?

_____
_____
_____
_____
_____
_____
_____
_____
_____
_____
_____
_____
_____

CONCLUSION

ENGAGE

"To each comes in their lifetime a special moment when they are figuratively tapped on the shoulder and offered the chance to do a very special thing; unique to them and fitted to their talents. What a tragedy if that moment finds them unprepared or unqualified for that which could have been their finest hour."
-Winston Churchill

Let me finish by telling you that this is just the beginning of your journey to recapture your sovereignty. When I founded Order of Man in March 2015, I did so believing that there was a gap between what we know we should be doing and what we actually do. This gap represents the greatest threat to the control and power you ultimately have over your life. That power and control is merely potential at this point.

Every man is born with something great inside him. Most men go to their graves without uncovering what that greatness is. It remains dormant and hidden from him and the world that could have benefited so much if only he would have had the strength to engage in the battle for his heart and mind.

Too many men seem so willing to give up that power and dis-engage from the battle they were born to fight. They rationalize, justify, and lie about why that's the case, but deep down in their hearts they know—they can feel it in every ounce of their being. Rather than advance in that battle, they retreat and attempt to mask what could potentially alter the course of their life.

This retreat is a combination of fear, social conditioning, and ignorance. Some men are aware of the battle and are too scared to do anything about it. Others have been carrying out conscious and subconscious orders so long that they forget they have a say in the matter. And some aren't aware at all and remain in a perpetual cycle of mediocrity and complacency.

You cannot possibly be the complacent man, or you wouldn't have picked up a copy of this book. If you're the man who has been carrying out orders without question for far too long, you now know you have more power than you've previously given yourself credit for.

If you're the man who is filled with fear about what this journey of sovereignty will mean, what it will change, and what you'll have to remove from your life, good. That fear, like I mentioned earlier, is the indicator that you're about to do something that is going to push you outside your comfort zone and ultimately test your mettle as a man.

The last thing I want regarding this book is for you to finish it, close it, set it on your shelf, and never implement anything you learned. This book's message can act as the catalyst for change and the operating system by which you live your life . . . if you choose to let it.

That is the choice you're left with now. Do you put this book down, check it off the list, and get motivated for the next week or so? Or do you permanently transform your life with an understanding that whether or not you like it, you're already in the battle?

But what a noble and honorable battle it is. In a world that tries to distort the reality of what makes a man a man, you have the ability to become a powerful pillar of strength and masculinity in your home, your business, your community, and the world.

Sure, you can retreat and revert back to the way things have always been. I'm sure no one will notice. Or you can live by the statement made by Robert Jordan: "There is one rule, above all others, for being a man. Whatever comes, face it on your feet."

So, where do you go from here?

You start by understanding that this book is not designed to tell you what exactly you should be doing with your life. That's up to you to determine, not me. This is simply a medium for equipping you with enough information to make your own decisions and choose your own path. If I laid it all out for you with the pages of this book, what right would I have to say that this is a journey of your own sovereignty?

Sovereignty isn't about doing what others expect you to do or what you "should" be doing. It's about making your own choices and carving out your own path. What you have in your hands is the foundational framework for building a life you and those you are responsible for can be proud of.

I've highlighted the battle we're fighting. I've shed light on our mission here as men. I've given you a valuable Code of Conduct that will help you on your way. You're now armed with the Battle Plan that will allow you to set your plans and desires into motion.

What you do with this information is entirely up to you. What you need to understand, however, is that the only thing that separates ordinary men from extraordinary men is the decision to be extraordinary and the grit and perseverance to carry it out.

I urge you to take what you know now, read it, study it, internalize it, and live it. Understand that this battle never ends, and you, potentially for the first time in your life, are becoming the soldier you were designed to be. It takes time. It takes patience. It takes resilience.

You will face hardships on your journey. You will have to let go of some thoughts, behaviors, and people who are holding you back.

Some will mock, ridicule, and leave you. You will be tempted to slip into default mode and pull the blindfold back over your eyes.

I could close out this book by blowing smoke up your ass and telling you how wonderful everything will be now that you have all this incredible information. But that isn't reality. The reality is that the fight for your sovereignty is messy, exhausting, and bloody.

It's my hope, however, that you aren't looking for the path of least resistance but the opportunity to engage in the fight and the fortitude to see it through to the end. After all, it's our ability to answer the call of battle that makes us men.

PODCASTS

Order of Man
The Art of Charm
Art of Manliness
The Good Dad Project
The Great Man Podcast
Jocko Podcast
The MFCEO Project
Self-Made Man

WHAT NEXT?

I started this journey to reclaim my sovereignty over nine years ago. While there have been plenty of ups and downs, one thing has remained constant: the more I surround myself with other men who are on a similar path, the better off I am.

That said, when I began to reclaim my masculine power, it was very difficult to find other men who were interested in doing the same. It seemed the men I had previously found myself in company with were more interested in maintaining the status quo than they were in bucking the system. So I came up with a solution—an exclusive brotherhood of men who are all on the same journey as I am.

It's called the Iron Council (www.OrderOfMan.com/IronCouncil), and, as the name implies, inside this brotherhood, you'll find a council of men who are actively engaged in the processes and systems shared throughout this book. Many men think they have to go at it alone. While you may eventually find whatever it is you're looking for on your own, there is infinite power in banding together with other men who will give you guidance, support, direction, and the occasional kick in the ass. When you join the Iron Council, you'll have access to weekly sessions, participate in a fifteen-man Battle Team, complete weekly assignments, engage in weekly challenges, and interact in a customizable communication platform with hundreds of other men having thousands of conversations.

But more important than all that, you'll learn that you're not alone on this journey to reclaim your sovereignty and reap the benefits of the power that's found when men stand shoulder to shoulder in a common battle toward a common purpose. The men inside the Iron Council are rekindling relationships, connecting with their children, starting businesses, getting promotions, losing weight, and building their bank accounts. That said, I'm not interested in blowing smoke up your ass. The Iron Council works only if you work. As the adage goes, "You can lead a horse to water, but you can't make him drink."

You can tap into the Iron Council, pay a few bucks a month, and tell everyone you're part of something, but unless you're willing to put forth the effort, you'll likely experience the same results you always have. But if you can commit to join us with an open mind, step outside of your comfort zone, and do some things you wouldn't normally do, I have no doubt that you'll experience a transformation unparalleled at any other point in your life, like many of our members have.

The Iron Council is not the end-all, save-all, but it might just be the resource you need to kick-start your journey to sovereignty. Join us at www.OrderOfMan.com/IronCouncil. See you inside.